Stay Healthy

Using Your Inner Power

Foreword by Bob Proctor,

Author of the best-selling book
"You Were Born Rich"
And featured in, "The Secret"

Axel Menzefricke

Edited by: Elizabeth Thompson and Pat Moauro
Author's portrait by: James Gayler

Printed in Canada
First Printing November 2007
Second Printing June 2008

How to Contact the Author
Axel Menzefricke has built a reputation for giving thought-provoking, compassionate, and inspiring presentations before a wide variety of audiences to help people unleash their personal power.

Email: axelmenzefricke@gmail.com

ISBN: 1467973823
ISBN 13: 9781467973823

Stay Healthy
Using Your Inner Power to Heal

*Every truth passes through three stages before it
is recognized. In the first it is ridiculed;
in the second it is opposed; in the
third it is regarded as self-evident.*

Arthur Schopenhauer

Dedication

*This book is dedicated to
Michelle, Thomas, Kurt and Lydia
for all of their loving support and trust.*

Foreword

The first time I met Axel Menzefricke was on a Cruise ship in October 2007. Axel was among thousands of people seeking spiritual guidance and personal development to achieve growth and fulfillment in his life.

Axels' story on how he overcame serious health challenges and was left to raise three young children after his wife's passing from cancer is an inspirational one. He has been an eager student to learn all about physical wellness and personal success from numerous experts and considers himself now in perfect health.

For the past 45 years I have been driven by the burning desire to understand what exactly it was that changed in me and to teach it to others. I see in Axel the same burning desire to teach the message that to acquire good health or prosperity and wealth requires similar if not the same attitude and behaviour. I know from personal experience that every successful person had to pass through and overcome incredible personal challenges.

The information and knowledge in this book is a compilation of wisdom from many different experts including Dr Joseph Murphy, Napoleon Hill and Deepak Chopra to name a few. They were re-arranged in an order that makes it easy to put to practical use and can work for anyone, anywhere, at anytime. He certainly offers nuances from his own personal experiences that will inspire your hopes and wishes to make the difference between success and failure in your life.

There is one word that I use in all of my seminars – praxis. Praxis is the integration of belief with behaviour. You can read this book from cover to cover and say that you know what Axel is talking about and believe what he is saying to be true. However, if you don't use the information to improve your quality of life, it can serve you only through application and use. Merely reading and passing judgment on it, either way, will in no way benefit you. I want to strongly suggest that you read this book with one view in mind: how you will use it to improve the quality of your life.

This book is for those who are looking to break through to a whole new level of physical well-being and abundance and for the person who is as I was many years ago, "sick and tired" of being broke and sick and tired. It is a shortcut to the proven information which when studied, understood and applied, will make you healthy and wealthy beyond your dreams.

This is a great and inspiring read!

Bob Proctor

Author of the best-selling book, "You Were Born Rich" and Featured in, "The Secret."

Contents

Acknowledgements

Thomas and Kurt, my sons, my pride and joy! Thank you for your youth, your inspiration and your valuable suggestions. You have wisdom far beyond your years.

Michelle, my daughter! You are very special in my life. Thank you for your never-ending support to help me rewrite my rough words, for proof reading this whole project and finishing it the day before you gave birth to your first child, my lovely first grandchild Anastasia Grace.

Lydia, my life partner! You are always encouraging and supportive when I needed you. Thank you for your unwavering support, love and kindness. I am blessed to have you in my life, I love you.

To my dear friend Elizabeth Thompson, thank you for your continuous effort to give help and advice. With all of your busy schedules, I really appreciate your following through when I needed you.

A sincere thank you to Pat Moauro, a new and special friend with your amazing style unlike any other. So full of wisdom and inspiration that I am blessed to know you, and privileged to call you a friend.

Disclaimer

The author of this book does not dispense medical advice or prescribe the use of any technique as a form of treatment for physical or medical problems without the advice of a physician, either directly or indirectly. The intent of the author is only to offer information of a general nature to help you in your quest for emotional and spiritual well-being. If you use any of the information in this book for yourself, which is your constitutional right, the author assumes no responsibility for your actions.

The author is not a medical doctor and has no formal medical training. This book is not intended to provide medical advice, diagnose illness, or in any way attempt to practice medicine. It is not intended to replace personal medical care from a licensed health care practitioner. Doing anything recommended in this book must be at your own risk. The author, publisher, and distributors present this information for educational purposes only. This book is based on, and inspired by, a true story and personal experience. Much of it comes from the author's memory and best recollection of events. Some information comes from manuscripts mentioned in the back of the book under References. The author is forced to include this disclaimer due to the litigious nature of today's world, and the expected attacks, criticisms, and attempts to suppress or discredit this work.

Introduction

You cannot be truthful if you are not courageous.
You cannot be loving if you are not courageous.
You cannot be trusting if you are not courageous.
You cannot inquire into reality if you are not courageous.
Hence courage comes first, and everything else follows.

Osho

YOU MAY BE SEEKING some certainty, a creed, somewhere to belong, or someone to rely upon. You come here out of your fear. You have two choices: Close your eyes and become dogmatic, in which case, you become like the proverbial ostrich burying your head in the sand, unable to change your life. Or you may choose to live in freedom, become aware of what's going on and take responsibility for the results in your life.

Throughout my life, I've faced the same obstacles, illnesses, and challenges as other people. However, I was fortunate enough to meet people who supported me in my efforts to open myself up to unconventional ways of overcoming those obstacles.

Diagnosed with colon cancer when I was 35, I had the malignant polyps removed, only to have the cancer metastasize (spread) to my liver six months later. Reflecting on the death of my father from liver cancer just

10 years earlier, when he was 60 years old, I realized that I faced the same fate at age 35. I also realized that my attitude and thinking patterns were similar to those of my father.

I decided to take anger management classes, alternative healing methods, lectures and seminars. By reading books from Dr. Wayne W. Dyer, Louise L. Hay, and Marianne Williamson, I discovered my spiritual path. The cancer disappeared and never came back. I want to share my lessons with you and guide you to use your power to heal yourself, and create the life you want.

Axel Menzefricke, ACS
Toronto
May 2008

*"The doctor of the future will give no medication,
but will interest his patients in the care
of the human frame, in diet,
and in the cause and
prevention of disease.*

Thomas Alva Edison

Chapter 1

What is Health?

Health is not a condition of matter, but of Mind.

Mary Baker Eddy — Science and Health

HEALTH IS A NATURAL STATE of consciousness. It is neither easy nor difficult. Good health is not an effort; hence, it can't be easy or difficult. It is simply natural; like your breathing, like your heartbeat. Health is your very being. Most people on this planet are born in perfect health. However, outside circumstances can change this state of being very quickly.

In western civilization, this state of being healthy has become almost impossible to maintain. A ruling element in society hinders our full enjoyment of health and wellness. This societal element conditions people in such a way that good health becomes almost impossible to maintain, and illness or discomfort is made to appear the norm. We are continually bombarded by the media (television, radio, newspapers, and magazines) with messages telling us that every normal person must have a medical cabinet stocked with assorted remedies just in case we suddenly feel some sort of discomfort or unease. The implication is that discomfort or disease is normal and to be expected at any time.

Each of us is given but one life, and we can only live it once. Each life holds no promises or guarantees, only possibilities and potential. Each person has the right and the privilege to pursue his or her highest potential. This pursuit is the true wellness journey.

Medicine tells us that *health* is the greatest goal of life. However, I believe that life's greatest goal is to fulfill the purpose for which you were meant to fulfill on your life's journey. Each of us came here with a purpose. Find your purpose and live in harmony with it. In fact, good health may lull us into complacency and weaken our interest and resolve in attaining our greatest goal

Academics tell us that the use of *knowledge* is the highest order of living. But many who claim wisdom fail the test of true greatness: What will others remember you for after you finish this lifetime?

Politicians say the quest for *liberty* is our supreme calling, claiming that we yearn for freedom and the pursuit of happiness more than anything else. But no matter how much freedom we may enjoy, this will not give us the benefits of the ultimate quest the quest to achieve our greatest potential. The goal is to be able to thrive in slavery as well as freedom.

Capitalists say *economic freedom* is our highest calling. Yet economic freedom and wealth does not necessarily equal supreme happiness. Rather, the greatest attainment is possible for both the rich and the poor.

Religion tells us that our greatest possession is *faith* - faith in God, in ourselves, or in our fellow humans. Sadly, the pursuit of faith has a questionable history filled with wars and oppression, and relatively little peace and personal compassion. In the name of faith, atrocities have been committed on large parts of society. Faith, alone, is not the supreme attainment of humanity.

What is the loving thing to do?

I would argue that the supreme attainment is the daily practice of the greatest of the non-negotiable laws of wellness, what I call the Law of Unconditional Loving. Unconditional, nonjudgmental loving is our goal, life's highest and most rewarding pursuit.

Some people claim that it is unattainable and outside the reach of human capability. But unconditional loving is indeed possible when we are willing to ask ourselves one question: "What is the loving thing to do?" Asked consistently and with courage, this question can transform a life, save a marriage, shape a child, reignite a career, and even change the world.

When we can answer this question we will find the supernatural power of living. We gain access to our higher intelligence. Some people call it God; however, it doesn't matter what you call it. Every person has access to it.

The more we align ourselves with the principles found in the Laws of Wellness, to that extent our higher potential will be released within and through us, enabling us to come closer to our Divine Design. We must complete the task we came here to perform. Each person has a special talent, skill or ability that is unique to him or her. Find out what your special talent is and integrate it into your life's pursuit.

The highest expression of Divine Design is the applied love found in loving relationships between people. Not the erotic love we see on television or in the movies, but love rooted in the decision to serve. It is a dynamic state of consciousness, a giving, creative flow, and harmony. We accept the human condition as perfectly imperfect. And we choose to love, regardless of any conditions.

I have seen cancer respond to the decision to love; and I have personally experienced such a response following my cancer diagnosis. After a sincere and thorough effort at forgiveness, with the help of an anger management class, I decided to love those around me (and myself), as best I could, without any conditions. Suddenly I saw the cancer and many other physical ailments in a totally different light.

I want to keep the information in this book as simple as possible because this is not being written for the medical community, scientists, or researchers. They may or may not believe or agree with what I say anyway. Of course, they too have feelings and opinions, which they may not always be able to express freely. This book is written in plain English so that you can understand it and draw hope, energy and benefit into your life.

Admittedly, everything I say in this book is not taken from medical textbooks but based on my own experiences. My conclusions and statements of fact are only my own opinions. Factual experiences in my life are valid only for me and may not be valid for anyone else. Nevertheless, I feel that I have knowledge which I can pass on to you, so that you can change your life, as I have changed mine.

I don't take credit for the incredible wisdom and philosophy in this book. Most of the information and advice came to me through books I have read, tapes I have listened to and workshops I have attended. I have studied this information and applied it to my life, so that you can change your life, as I have changed mine. Most of my knowledge came from the books mentioned on the last pages under References. I obtained permission to write certain phrases and quotes and am eternally grateful to have witnessed such powerful wisdom.

Interestingly, medical science always presents things as fact, when it is actually presenting an opinion, based on currently available data and information. Throughout history, medical "facts" have been proven untrue repeatedly. Therefore, we can assume that what is considered fact today is merely an opinion and may eventually be relegated to yesterday's theory.

Many look to the medical industry as the only source of truth when it comes to health, illness, and disease. It uses words like credible scientific evidence, scientifically tested, scientifically proven. The fact is that medical professionals are really presenting theories, which constantly change.

Here are some examples of "medical facts" that have been proven to be wrong:

- Bloodletting was known to cure most illnesses. Now it is considered totally ineffective.
- Margarine was considered much healthier than butter. Now research suggests that the exact opposite is true.
- Eggs were considered very bad because of high cholesterol. Now research suggests that they are not bad at all; they are actually healthy for your body.
- The medical community claimed that baby formula was much better than breast milk for children. Now the exact opposite is shown to be true.
- Milk was recommended for coating the stomach and alleviating stomach ulcers. Now this is discouraged because it has been found to aggravate ulcers.

- At one time, medical science stated that diet had absolutely no effect on disease or illness. Now we are told that diet has a huge effect on the prevention and cause of disease. Note the current concern about the effects of poor diet on young children and teenagers with obesity.

- Medical science once believed that removal of tonsils and appendix improved health and should be done to virtually everyone. Now the medical community has reversed that theory.

- Another example of where medical facts have been reversed involves the diet industry. First, a low calorie diet was the only correct way to lose weight. Then experts said, "It's not the calories, but the amount of fat you consume that will determine your weight." Now the word of the day is "It's not the calories, and it's not the fat — it's the carbohydrates that cause obesity." The fact is, nobody really knows.

- The most obvious example of all: thousands of drugs have been approved by the FDA because they are scientifically proven to cure or prevent disease, in addition to having been declared safe. However, years later, many are taken off the market because they are newly proven not to cure or prevent disease. Indeed, some have such terrible adverse side effects that they are simply too dangerous for people to use.

I'm saddened when I see doctors on TV stating things as fact, when they should be prefacing their comments with such phrases as: "It appears, based on the current research we have….;" or "It seems that…;" or again, "We believe this to be true."

Unfortunately, this is seldom heard. Whatever medical doctors say is accepted as being absolutely true. What any one else says about health, illness, or disease does not carry the same weight and credibility as the words of a medical doctor. I disagree. Medical doctors are trained to prescribe drugs or cut out parts of a person's anatomy (perform surgery). Generally, they are not trained to prevent disease. Most importantly, they have little or no training in or exposure to treatment other than drugs or surgery.

Imagine the government's highest medical authority making the following statement:

> "Today we have more information and knowledge about the cure and prevention of disease than ever before in the history of mankind. The advancements that have been made in just the last few years have given us new insights about the treatment and prevention of virtually all illness and disease, making it safe to reach two major conclusions: (1) even though just ten years ago we thought we knew the proper treatments of illness, we now know just how little we knew back then; and (2) with these revolutionary breakthroughs in technology, virtually all illness and disease should be wiped out in America within the next ten years. We are on the verge of being in a place where a person will never be sick. And if you do get sick, your doctor will be able to cure you of your illness in a matter of days. We have virtually reached the pinnacle of medical knowledge."

Sounds exciting, doesn't it? Wow! Let's celebrate! We have reached the pinnacle of medical knowledge. We know all there is to know about the cure and prevention of disease. In just ten years, because of medical science, sickness will be eliminated in America.

But what if the speech was given in 1902, not 2008? Interesting, isn't it? In 1902, the people of the day believed they knew all there was to know about the cure and prevention of disease. We look back at them and see how little they knew. Twenty years from now, people will look at us and see how little we really knew about the cure and prevention of disease. Today we laugh at the thought of using bloodletting to cure disease. Well, 50 years from now, people will laugh when they look at some of the treatments we use in our attempts to cure illness.

Please note: there are virtually no medical facts. There are only medical opinions. You need to choose the opinion that makes the most sense for you.

As well, everything written in this book pertains only to illness and disease. *It does not apply to accident victims or personal injury.* If you are in a car accident with a ruptured liver or kidney, or broken bones, you would be wise to get to the nearest hospital emergency room fast and have a medical professional take care of you.

Think of the things that make you happy,
Not the things that make you sad;
Think of the fine and true in mankind,
Not its sordid side and bad;
Think of the blessings that surround you,
Not the ones that are denied;
Think of the virtues of your friendships,
Not the weak and faulty side;
Think of the hopes that lie before you,
Not the waste that lies behind;
Think of the treasures you have gathered,
Not the ones you've failed to find;
Think of the service you may render,
Not of serving self alone;
Think of the happiness of others,
And in this you'll find your own!

Robert E. Farley

Chapter 2

Why are we Sick?

Health is a state of complete physical, mental, and social well-being, and not merely the absence of disease and infirmity.

World Health Organization

WE SPEND MORE MONEY on healthcare than ever before, we take more drugs than before, and yet we are sicker than before. As mentioned in the previous chapter, there are actually no medical facts as such. Everything is simply an opinion based on current available information. Many "medical facts" that are presented are actually opinions which often lead to drugs and medication that can result in the greatest profit.

If information about the prevention, cure, or diagnosis of disease has no benefit for the pharmaceutical and medical industry, that "medical fact" will not be presented at all. Instead, it will be debunked and suppressed.

Over the years, the pharmaceutical industry has come up with different theories about why people get sick. First, it was bacteria and germs.

The super wonder drugs of the day were antibiotics, which were declared as a method to cure all illnesses and eliminate disease forever. The theory was that all disease was caused by germs, especially bacteria. This theory has been proved wrong. Ever stronger antibiotics are developed, yet people continue to be sick.

The next theory was that viruses were the cause of all disease. Unfortunately, few people know that antibiotics have no effect on viruses, and doctors continue to prescribe antibiotics routinely. People have been brainwashed into thinking that antibiotics are needed when they feel sick; so when they're a bit under the weather, they head to their doctor and demand antibiotics. The doctor, who is in a business to serve his or her patient as a customer, has to make the customer happy and prescribes the antibiotic. If the doctor does not, the patient will simply find another doctor who will prescribe it. The government estimates that half of the one hundred million antibiotic prescriptions written each year are totally unnecessary.

Keep in mind that drug companies really do not want to cure disease as they claim. If they came up with a cure, they would be out of business. Think of herpes. Herpes is a virus. Television commercials proclaim daily, "There is no cure for herpes." Therefore, in order to suppress the symptoms, take our wonderful drug everyday for the rest of your life.

But what if there were a cure? What if we heard an advertisement saying: "Here is a cure for herpes, simply take this herb for thirty days and you will never have a herpetic breakout ever again. By the way, this herb is not patented, and it only costs three dollars." Drug companies would lose billions of dollars in profits. Stock prices would plummet. There is no incentive to cure herpes. The incentive is to keep you brainwashed into believing there is no cure, and the only solution to the "symptoms" is drugs.

Remember, the FDA in the U.S. and the drug companies work hand-in-hand. If I happen to know a cure for herpes, I cannot say so. Because if I say this, I am making a medical claim and, according to the FDA, I am breaking the law. Even if what I say is true, I am still breaking the law. Federal agents will arrest me, throw me in jail, and confiscate any papers I have, suppress the information, and outlaw it because there is no "credible scientific evidence". They will issue press releases and statements of "fact" that I am a charlatan and have no scientific evidence to substantiate what I am saying. Unfortunately, that's how the system works.

You need to be aware of the questionable intentions and activities of the pharmaceutical industry, the FDA, the FTC, the crooked charities and foundations, the associations, and the politicians. Isn't it strange that you are never informed of the identity of the directors or major shareholders of these organizations? These individual people hide behind corporations, trusts, and a maze of legal structures so that their true identities remain hidden. If the money trail were followed, it would shock you to find that it leads to a small group of billionaires from around the world who are pulling the strings.

Let's return to the main point. Why do you get sick? Is it germs? Is it bacteria? Is it viruses? Is it genetics? Just think about it. You don't catch cancer. Your body develops cancer. I created the cancer in my body in the same way my father created the cancer in his body, through negative attitude and faulty thinking patterns. You don't catch diabetes. Your body develops diabetes. You don't catch headaches, or back pain, or PMS, or impotence. These are all "medical conditions" that are developed in the body. They aren't germs, viruses or bacteria.

Most illness is, in fact, self-inflicted and not passed down genetically. What is passed down is the attitude that runs in a family, passed down from one generation to the next. Drugs are not the answer. You don't have a headache because you have an aspirin deficiency.

The question is: Why do human beings have so much illness?

You have to realize that being sick is not normal: it is not the body's natural state. Your body is not supposed to get sick. Animals don't get heart attacks. I repeat animals *never* get heart attacks. Animals don't get cancer, diabetes, arthritis, or virtually any of the common human diseases, except, of course, when they are in captivity. When they are under human care and get vaccine injections, drugs, and processed food, animals contract many of the diseases that humans are riddled with. My personal answer to the question is the following.

Any physical discomfort or so-called symptom is a physical message or lesson that the person is misperceiving something.

Alternatively, the person may have a faulty attitude. It might have been beneficial in the past, during childhood, for example, but it has been carried over into adulthood by mistake. If you are willing to learn the lesson, and go within your psyche, preferably through meditation, which will be addressed in a later chapter, you can find the cause of the illness. However, if you ignore the lesson and choose the easy route by taking medication in the beginning stages of the discomfort, you will soon experience a progressive worsening of your symptoms.

I created the cancer in my body the same way my father created his cancer in his body – by default. I nourished a deep resentment towards my childhood, carrying my childhood view of my upbringing into adulthood, and creating a total misperception of what happened during my early years. My father had a similar misperception about his childhood and created his cancer using the same type of thought pattern. Unfortunately, he didn't get the guidance necessary to lead him out of his incorrect thought patterns. I consider myself fortunate to have received the right kind of guidance; it helped me to overcome the cancer. Books with incredible wisdom were given to me. People with special knowledge and coaching abilities stepped into my path to direct me where I needed to go. And now it is my turn to guide you now with the contents of this book, so that you may help a loved one – a friend, a relative, or yourself – overcome the physical challenges you were meant to overcome.

Look to your health; and if you have it, praise God, and value it next to a good conscience; for health is the second blessing that we mortals are capable of, a blessing that money cannot buy.

Izaak Walton

Chapter 3

How to Live Healthy All the Days of Your Life!

Natural forces within us are the true healers of disease.

Hippocrates

AT THIS MOMENT you may have some illness or disease such as cancer, diabetes, or a less severe condition. Alternatively, you may claim to be "healthy." If you claim to be healthy, you might still experience the occasional headache, pain, indigestion, cold, flu, heartburn, and so on. Most people believe that these medical conditions are "normal." They are not.

Healthy people have little, if any, body odour. They have no bad breath, no foot odour. Their urine and stools do not smell bad. They sleep soundly, they have no skin rashes or dandruff, they are not depressed or stressed, they rarely get colds, flu, heartburn, or general aches and pains. Truly healthy people are full of energy and vitality, and never have to take prescription or nonprescription drugs because they never have symptoms that would require them to take a drug.

Unfortunately, our healthcare system has successfully brainwashed us to believe that as we get older, it is "normal" to be on some sort of medication. This simply is not true. Nevertheless, there is an inordinate amount of illness. In fact, at this moment, you are either: a) very sick; b) somewhat sick; or c) about to get sick. A truly healthy person is very rare in our society.

The good news is there is a way out, and it does not rely on prescribed medications or surgical procedures. Before you are on the journey to recovery, or better health, or simply an increase in energy and well-being, you have to be willing to adjust your belief system on how you perceive illness and diseases.

Our current healthcare system is very successful in brainwashing you and making you believe that you are not responsible for having discomfort or disease. They tell you: "It is the bad food you eat, the tap water you drink, the polluted air you breathe, the stressful job you perform, the bad UV rays of the sun, and dozens of other reasons why you get sick." I don't believe that any of this is true.

I am convinced that any discomfort or disease is a lesson from which you can learn.

I truly believe that any symptom in your body is trying to teach you a lesson. In other words, *the symptom in your physical body is telling your mind that you are misperceiving something.*

Your headache is *not* caused by the absence of Aspirin. Your cold is *not* caused by the bad weather or bacteria or viruses, or the absence of vitamins. You did *not* inherit diabetes genetically, because it runs in your family, and you did *not* get cancer or any other disease, because your parents or other relatives have had it.

If you find the real cause for your discomfort or disease and are willing to take responsibility for it, you have a very good chance of eliminating it and preventing it from ever recurring. This kind of thinking or belief system is considerably different from what our current healthcare system is trying to make you believe. In a later chapter, I will explain in more detail how to find the real cause of your disease or symptoms. For now, I recommend that you seek proper healthcare from a professional healthcare provider who does not use drugs or surgery.

Since every person is different, and every condition is different, you need to have a knowledgeable person examine you and give you appropriate care. Keep in mind that all healthcare providers have different backgrounds and experiences, and may have different opinions about the course of action that is best for you. It is wise to get opinions from several people. It is most beneficial to have faith in your gut feelings.

The following is a list of my personal recommendations for taking your first step. You have probably heard them before. They are likely only a reminder of what you already know.

1. **Eat more fresh fruits and vegetables.**
2. **Eat more fish and less meat,** regardless whether it's red or white meat.
3. **Get more natural sunlight.** Your body needs sunlight. Go for a walk in the sun as often as you can. Thirty minutes a day in the sun promotes incredible health benefits. Remember, the sun creates growth in plants and all other living creatures. The purpose of the sun is not to make us sick or cause illness. Don't be misled by the medical establishment. The sun is good for you. It is absolutely needed in moderation, as is everything else in your life. I don't use sunglasses or sunscreens, and I don't get sun burns either.
4. **Eat an apple a day.**
5. **Sweat.** Your body is designed to sweat. It is the natural way to eliminate toxins. If you don't sweat, toxins build up in your system. The best way to sweat is in a dry sauna.
6. **Eat raw nuts and seeds.** Raw means uncooked. Buy nuts and seeds in the shell and snack on them throughout the day.
7. **Stay away from diet sodas.** The artificial sweeteners used, such as aspartame, cause a variety of medical symptoms. The idea that diet sodas have fewer calories and are good for weight control is a lie. The exact opposite is true. Diet sodas will actually make you gain weight, as well as make you depressed.

8. **Eliminate aspartame and monosodium glutamate as best as you can.**

9. **Stay away from anything with "fat free," "sugar free," "low carbs," or "net carbs" on the label.** These foods have harmful chemicals in them. Diet or protein shakes, vitamins, and food supplements fall into the same category. Our digestive system is not able to absorb these nutrients regardless of how much or little we pay for them. If you feel any improvement after taking the supplements, it's merely a "placebo effect."

10. **Do breathing exercises.** One good exercise I recommend and use for myself is the following. When I am walking, I count my steps. When I am in rhythm with walking and counting, I breathe in deeply to a count of 4. I keep the breath in for a count of 16. Then, I breathe out slowly to a count of 8, imagining that I am blowing out a candle.

11. **Speak powerful words.** The thoughts in your mind create the words you speak. The words you speak create your actions. Your actions create your experiences. Thus, if you don't like the experiences in your life, you must change your thoughts. Positive affirmations spoken out loud can create miracles in your life.

12. **Stretch.** When your body is flexible and in harmony, energy flows easily, and blockages do not occur. When energy flows, it is hard for illness and disease to take hold and manifest. Take yoga lessons, or Pilates, or any other kind of stretching on a regular basis. Throughout the day, I place my hands on a counter, table, banister or railing, pushing my whole body up and stretching my spine, until my feet come off the ground. It feels good, and it keeps my spine elastic.

13. **Listen to relaxing music.** Music has a powerful effect on our physiology. There are CDs that have been developed especially to produce stunning health benefits. In a few minutes, the music can relieve stress, relax muscles, and create a feeling of well-being. These CDs can be listened to anytime and anywhere, even while driving a car. They are perfect for a five- to fifteen-minute afternoon relaxation and recharging session.

14. **Do Spring Forest Qigong.** Qigong is similar to tai chi in that it is a series of movements that stimulate energy flow and has many health benefits. I recommend that you go to the following web site if you wish to learn more: www.LearningStrategies.com/Qigong.

15. **Fast.** For information on fasting, see Kevin Trudeau's excellent website at: www.naturalcures.com.

16. **Smile.** There are more muscles concentrated in your face than in any other part of the body. The physical act of smiling strengthens the immune system and releases endorphins from the brain, making you feel better. Make it a habit to notice if you are smiling or not. Smile for no reason and do it often.

17. **Give and get hugs**. Human contact is necessary for life. Our immune systems are strengthened when we hug another human being, a pet, or a tree for that matter. It is a good habit and provides increased health.

18. **Avoid using a cell phone while driving a motor vehicle**. Driving is stressful enough. When you are talking on a cell phone while driving, the amount of physical stress your body is experiencing can be as much as ten times greater than normal. If you are unable to pull over, return the call later.

19. **Be thankful.** Thoughts are energy. When you wake up in the morning, take a moment to be thankful for the day. Before you eat a meal, take a moment to be thankful for the food. Before you go to bed, be thankful for the people and experiences you have had during the day. Living a life of thankfulness creates happiness, peace, and harmony.

20. **Laugh.** Laughing is one of the most powerful and beneficial things you can do. Laughing stimulates the entire immune system and elevates depression. Laugh, even if you have nothing to laugh about. You will feel better and be healthier.

21. **Add living plants to your home.** Plants add oxygen to the air, balance the energy in the space, and are incredibly beneficial to human health. When you fill your house with plants and flowers, you will feel the difference.

22. **Get out of debt.** Financial pressures cause a massive increase in stress, which leads to disease, marriage breakup, family collapse, and other traumatic events. There are many organizations that can assist you in managing, reducing, and eliminating your debt load. Freedom from financial worry can cause you to be happier and healthier.

23. **Get a pet.** Research indicates that pet owners live longer with fewer diseases. Pets give unconditional love. The process of being loved and giving love strengthens our immune system, reduces stress, and has a variety of other emotional and physical benefits.

24. **Sleep eight hours.** Ideally, get a full eight hours of solid, deep, restful sleep every night without sleeping pills. If you are dependent on sleeping pills, learn how to meditate, so that you can eliminate them. Inquire at your local health food store for a practitioner who can teach you. Once you know how to count yourself down to a deep sleep, you can do it any time you want to. In Ayurvedic medical practice, it is believed that there are certain bodily cycles that are conducive for certain activities. Going to bed at 10:00pm and arising at 6:00am appears to allow the best rest and rejuvenation, and results in the maximum amount of energy throughout the following day.

25. **Use aromatherapy.** Smells have a powerful effect on our body. Essential oils have many health benefits besides giving a pleasant aroma. Inquire in your local health food store for an aromatherapy expert who can help you choose essential oils and aromas that will yield you the most benefits.

26. **Take a 15-minute afternoon break.** A 15-minute relaxation break, ideally using special music or relaxation CDs, allows the body and mind to unwind and rejuvenate. This procedure can increase metabolism, and relieve stress, anxiety, tension, and depression. It will allow you to feel more centred, and it will provide increased physical energy.

27. **Cook.** When you cook food from scratch, you take a much needed mental break. When you create something with your hands, you benefit emotionally and physically.
28. **Have more sex.** There are many books on how you can rejuvenate your sex life with your partner. If you don't have a partner, masturbate.
29. **Eat snacks.** Fresh fruits and raw vegetables can tide you over between mealtimes. Don't go hungry.
30. **Use foot orthotics.** These promote general health and can eliminate foot, joint, and back pain.
31. **Commit reckless acts of kindness.** Make it a habit to be kind to everyone you meet. The act of showing kindness has been shown to stimulate the body's immune system and gives us a greater sense of peace and harmony. Remember, too, that what goes around comes around.
32. **Reduce TV time.** The images on TV are negative and stress-invoking. That alone should encourage you to turn off the television. But the number one reason I believe you should avoid television is that two-thirds of all the ads you see are for drugs. When you watch TV, you are setting yourself up to be brainwashed into believing that drugs are the answer. Statistics show that more than 90 percent of North Americans believe that health is directly related to the amount of drugs you consume. They believe if parents do not administer drugs to a sick child immediately, they are being bad parents. These ads are so effective that people who seldom see a doctor are now asking their doctor for specific drugs. No one is immune to the power of these ads. I know I am not, and that's why I rarely watch TV.
33. **Write down goals.**
    Here you have my own basic list from which you can choose what is beneficial to you and what is not. It would be silly to believe that a person could do all these things all of the time. Ideally, do as many as you can, as often as you can. Doing even

a little bit is better than none at all. For example, if you don't like pets, ignore that part. Forcing something into your life that goes against your nature can't be beneficial. But when you write down a list of goals you want to accomplish, the likelihood of achieving them is much higher than if you have not written them down.

For more information, go to Kevin Trudeau's website at www.naturalcures.com

Forgiveness is the key to emotional healing.

*Make peace with all those who have wronged you and
forgive yourself for your own mistakes.*

*And to heal the spirit, find a way to commune with God "as you understand
Him to be." Make that connection in the way that feels right to you,
and a deep peace will fill your soul. Once you drink from the
waters of the living spirit, you will never thirst again.*

Douglas Bloch - I Am With You Always

Chapter 4

The Purpose of Meditation

*The Universe is the result of the meditation of
God. You are a spiritual being, living in a spiritual
Universe, governed by spiritual laws. You are here
to become conscious of, experience and express
the Divine - which you already are.*

Marilyn Lindstrom - The Voice From Inner Space

ANY DOMINANT THOUGHT that you continue to hold ultimately turns into a belief. Your beliefs will direct your attitude and actions. Your attitude and actions will create the results in your life. If you are not happy with the results in your life, you have to change some part of your thinking process.

Many of your beliefs serve you extremely well: you have thoughts that harmonize with the knowledge of your inner spirit, and thoughts that match your desires. But some of your beliefs do not serve you well: these may be thoughts about your inadequacy or your unworthiness, or thoughts of guilt and shame.

Your belief system has taken shape over time, starting in early childhood. However, what was valid and helpful to you as a little child, may not be valid and helpful to you as an adult. Fears, worries, and other negative thoughts carried over from youth, may be so deeply ingrained in your reality, that you may find the idea of making any conscious change difficult to imagine.

Even with the best of intentions, consciously changing your belief system in any direction is extremely difficult. However, by being willing to choose your thoughts deliberately, you can, in time, replace all destructive beliefs with life-giving beliefs. Using meditation, you can permanently change your beliefs much sooner and with less effort.

It is easier for most people to clear their minds, having no thought, than it is to think pure, positive thoughts. When you quiet your mind, having no thoughts, you automatically eliminate resisting thoughts. At this state of consciousness, your vibrational level of energy is much higher than when you are at a level of conscious resistance.

Imagine a cork bobbing in a pail of water. The cork represents the place of high, pure, easy vibration that is natural to you. Now, imagine holding the cork down under the water. That is what resistance is like. And now imagine letting go of the cork – watch it quickly bob up to the surface.

Like the cork, naturally floating on the water's surface, it is natural for you to experience a high, pure, easy vibration, free of damaging resistance. And like the cork, if you are not doing something that holds you down under the water, you will bob right back up to the surface where you belong. In other words, you do not have to work at being in the high vibration that is natural to you, simply because it *is* natural to you.

But you *do* have to stop thinking the thoughts that cause you to lower your vibration. It is a matter of replacing your attention from the things that do not allow your cork to float, when you resist vibrating in harmony with what you really desire. If your thoughts are in harmony with what you desire, you will experience a natural state of thriving and wellbeing. You have to decide that nothing is more important than feeling good – that you are going to seek out the thoughts which make you feel better. Your cork floating is now the most important motivator in your life!

Look at the process of meditation as a shortcut to changing your beliefs. In meditation, there is an absence of thought. In the absence of thought, there is no resistance within you, and your cork bobs naturally to the surface.

The following true experience will demonstrate my point about the power of meditation. In November 1995, my wife passed away after a lengthy struggle with cancer. My youngest son Kurt was eleven years of age at the time. About five months after Kurt's mother died, a routine checkup at school showed that he had an abnormally high blood count in his urine – more than ten times the normal amount. The school nurse recommended an immediate consultation with an urologist. A few days later, Kurt and I saw an urologist who recommended inserting a catheter with a small camera attached to it into his urinary track to determine the reason for the blood in his urine. I could very well imagine how this process would affect an eleven-year-old boy and decided not to proceed with it.

From Louise Hay's book *Heal Your Body,* I knew that blood represents joy in our life. The loss of his mother five months earlier caused Kurt to lose a great deal of joy in his life. I sat down with him. We talked about the grieving process his brother and sister and I were going through. I told him it was normal to be sad and grief-stricken. I also told him that it was perfectly normal for young men to cry and to release tears of sadness, contrary to the common social understanding that boys don't cry.

I explained to him how to meditate, telling him that he could use the calm meditative state to experience feelings of sadness, loss, and despair. After we had meditated together and talked about it, we hugged each other and had a good cry. We did this twice a day for about a week; then I encouraged Kurt to do this on his own as often as he felt like it. Four weeks after we started the meditation session I sent him for an additional urine test; this time, the results were negative, and he had a normal level of blood in his urine.

I used the following meditation technique:

Begin the meditation by sitting in a quiet place where you are not likely to be interrupted. Wear comfortable clothing. It doesn't matter if you sit in a chair or on the floor, or even lie on your bed, unless you tend to fall asleep. The important thing is that your body is comfortable.

Now, close your eyes, relax, and breathe slowly. Draw air into your lungs, and then enjoy the comfortable release of that air. Your personal comfort here is very important. As your mind wanders, gently refocus on your breathing. In the beginning, this process will feel unnatural, and you will find your mind wandering to things you have been focusing on previously. When this happens, relax, breathe again, and try to release the thought by focusing on your inhalation and exhalation.

It is easier to quiet your mind if you choose small thoughts that do not have the potential for expanding into something interesting. You could mentally count down your breaths descending from three to one. Do this three times in a row and then breath normally. Now count yourself down from ten to one at a slow pace: ten, nine, and eight, deeper and deeper; seven, six, and five, deeper and deeper; four, three, two, and one, deeper and deeper. If you repeat this until all thoughts of resistance have gone, your vibration will naturally rise.

This is not a process where you work on your desires. Rather, this is a process of quieting your mind. While you are at it, any resistance will subside, and your state of vibration will rise to its natural, pure state.

As you quiet your mind, you may feel a sense of physical detachment. For example, you may feel twitches and itches beneath your skin. Or you feel an involuntary movement of your body or limbs, or your head may roll gently from side to side, or you may get the urge to yawn. Any or all of these sensations or movements are indicators that you are achieving a state of relaxation.

With more practice, your point of attraction will change. Things you have been asking for are now flowing gently into your experience. With enough practice, those higher frequencies will become so familiar to you that you will be able to reclaim them whenever you choose.

Over time, if you meditate regularly, you will become quite sensitive to the way the higher frequencies feel within your body. In other words, whenever you focus on something negative, you will be more likely to recognize it at the early, subtle stages before any negative experiences actually occur. And you will be able to easily change your resistant thoughts to maintain your balance.

As well as meditating, you can quiet your mind by listening to music that makes your heart sing; jogging in a beautiful place; petting your cat; walking your dog; and so on. There are many pleasant activities that cause a release of resistance and a rise in vibration. Often you are in your highest state while driving your car. The rhythm of the road, the distraction from what has been bothering you and the idea of going someplace new often cause you to leave behind thoughts of things that are bothering you. In this state, you may not recollect how you got to your destination. But driving with your subconscious mind is usually safer than with your cluttered conscious mind.

Your ultimate goal, whether you meditate or drive your car, is to release any thought that causes resistance so that you are in a place of pure, positive thought. It doesn't matter if you cannot completely quiet your mind — unless your mind is chattering about negative things. If you are softly thinking about pleasant things, it can be of great value.

The following is a meditation process which you can record with your own voice onto a tape or CD. Alternatively, someone can read it to you while you are in a relaxed state of mind. The guiding words for the following meditation were created by; Janet MacDonald and Jonathan Cramer from

www.scienceofhappiness.com

A Meditation

Imagine that you are walking down a country road. It is a sunny day. There is a cool breeze, and a few billowy clouds float lazily overhead. As you walk down this road, you know that you are on your way to meet your younger self, the part of you that holds a limiting belief about physical health and prosperity. As you walk, there is a path off to your right, a path through the forest, and as you walk into the woods and follow the path, you are aware of the sounds of these beautiful woods — the rustling of leaves overhead, the sounds of your footsteps, your easy breathing. And as the sunshine is filtered through the leaves and you smell the rich earth smells of the forest, you now repeat your positive belief about your physical health. (Repeat your own affirmation here.)

As you say this affirmation to yourself, notice how the colours, sounds and feelings here in these woods are intensified, so that you are now experiencing the wonderful abundant world around you and within you.

Up ahead you see a clearing, and as you get closer you see a tall oak tree standing in the middle of the clearing. And you know this tree is a symbol of strength and power. At the base is a bench where you can sit and enjoy this peaceful scene.

As you sit on this very comfortable bench, you rest your head against the tree. You can almost feel the life force coursing through the tree. And you know that the tree, like you, has deep roots that give it strength and stability as it draws nutrients up from the soil. Strong and flexible branches sway with the passing breezes and green leaves absorb the sunshine. Like the tree, you continue to grow and adapt to the ever-changing environment. You close your eyes as you rest by the tree, and your mind is at ease.

As you rest here, you sense someone watching from the safety of the forest. You calmly ask, "Who is there?" You notice a small child hiding on the edge of the clearing. You recognize this child as your younger self, the part that holds limiting beliefs about physical health and prosperity. And you tell the child, "I am from the future. I have come to thank you for doing your best to take care of me and to keep me safe."

The child walks out of the forest now and comes near, standing directly in front of you. You again thank the child for having your best interests at heart, for doing the very best he or she knew to protect you and keep you safe. Now ask that child what his or her positive intention has been with the limiting belief he/she has held during your lifetime. What does this child want for you that he/she perceives as positive? (Pause for about 30 seconds here.)

Now thank the child. Invite the child to sit on your lap. Again tell him/ her, "I come from your future. And because I have had many more experiences and learning, I now believe that it is possible for us to be in excellent health, be prosperous and to experience the abundance of the universe." Share your learning and understanding with the child now as you express your positive beliefs about good health and prosperity with this child through your thoughts and feelings. (Pause for about 30 seconds.)

Reassure the child that you will do everything in your power to assure the child's safety and security while you continue together to begin creating more healing and more abundance in your life. Let the child know that you want this to be a partnership as you begin to work together. (Pause for about 20 seconds here.)

Now, reach out, and as you embrace the child, pull him/her right into you as you become one. (Pause for about 10 seconds.)

Your life is now different as you honour the child within you. You continue to develop healthier and more productive beliefs about your own abilities to create healing, prosperity, and abundance in your life. Notice how it is different now. (Pause for about 10 seconds.)

As you leave the bench and the energizing aura of the oak tree and walk back down the path towards the road, you take with you the wonder and passion and curiosity of your childhood, combined with the strength and understanding of your adulthood.

You are now back on the road of your life. As you walk this road, notice that you are becoming aware of more opportunities on your life's road and that these opportunities come in many different disguises. You can choose the ones that are appropriate for you, knowing that opportunities surround you every day. With an emerging sense of purpose growing within you each day, you create healing and prosperity in your life through your thoughts and your actions, and you share this with each person that you meet.

Repeat the following affirmation: "I am deserving of love, joy, good health, and abundance. I am a magnet for all positive ideas and situations. My life is rich with opportunities and energizing experiences." (Pause for about 10 seconds.)

Take a moment now to create an image of the new life you desire for yourself. (Pause for about 20 seconds.)

In a moment this exercise will end. When you open your eyes you will be wide awake, feeling fine and in vibrant health, feeling better than before, experiencing even more of life's abundance in a spirit of thankfulness and appreciation.

Slowly open your eyes, take a deep breath, stretch, and notice how well and prosperous you feel!

Now remember the positive belief you have about your own health and prosperity. You deserve it. The universe is an abundant place. Whatever the positive belief is, say it to yourself with conviction. (Say your belief aloud). Say it again, and imagine how your life is different, now that this belief is fully active in your life.

I am still and know that I am a child of the healing power of the universe. It flows through me and into (name of person) to heal, renew, restore, and make well, healthy and whole, anything in his body, mind or soul that needs it.

The white light protects us, and I approach this person with love so that only the highest can come to either one of us. I let spirit direct my thoughts and actions to do what they need to do. The divine healing energy exchanged between us blesses us both for having come together today. Amen

Maggie Kelly
(spoken prior to a healing treatment)

Chapter 5

The Universal Healing Principle

ALL SCHOOLS OF HEALING have well-documented cases of most incredible cures. Since various schools of healing use vastly different methods to arrive at similarly incredible cures, there must be some underlying process that is common to all of them. And indeed there is. The common element is the organ of healing – your subconscious mind. And the common process is faith.

Before talking about healing, let me backtrack for a bit and talk about the power of your subconscious. Your subconscious mind has complete control of the functions, conditions, and sensations of your body. Your subconscious mind is constantly receptive to the power of suggestion. That's why it is so damaging to see the hundreds of medical advertisements on TV.

You have surely heard that symptoms of almost any disease can be induced in hypnotized people by suggestion. For example, a person in a hypnotic state can develop a high temperature, or chills according to the suggestion given. You can suggest to the person that he is paralyzed and cannot walk or move and it will be so. You can hold a cup of cold water under the nose of the hypnotized person and tell her, "This is full of ground pepper: smell it!" She will sneeze violently and repeatedly. What caused her to sneeze? Was it the water or the suggestion?

If someone tells you he is allergic to normal flour, and you place an empty glass in front of his nose, when he is in a hypnotic state, and tell him it is filled with flour, he will develop his usual allergic symptoms. This shows us that the cause of the symptoms is in the subconscious mind.

Curing the symptoms also takes place in the subconscious mind

Different schools of medicine, such as homeopathy, osteopathy, chiropractic, qigong, acupuncture, and naturopathy, all produce remarkable healing. So do the rites and ceremonies of different religious beliefs throughout the world. It is obvious that all of these healings are brought about through the subconscious mind – the only healer there is.

Notice how the subconscious mind heals a cut on your finger. It knows exactly how to do it. The doctor dresses the wound and says, "Nature heals it!" But "nature" is none other than your subconscious mind.

When I was diagnosed with liver cancer and decided to take an anger management class instead of the conventional treatment the doctors recommended, I learned how to quiet and calm myself, especially before bedtime. Every evening, before going to sleep, I affirmed, sometimes quietly and sometimes aloud, "Every cell, tissue, nerve and organ is now being made whole, pure, and perfect. My whole body is being restored to health and harmony." After six months, tests showed that the cancerous cells were no longer present.

I believe the most beneficial time to do this type of affirmation is before bedtime, because the kinetic action of the subconscious mind continues throughout the sleep time and has no conscious distractions hindering the process. Doing this kind of affirmation in the morning for the purpose of healing is likely to be interrupted by everyday activities

Notice that in thinking of harmony and perfect health, I did not refer to my condition by name. I strongly suggest that you stop talking about your ailments or giving them a name, especially in the hours leading up to sleep. You are giving them life by your attention and fear. Become a mental tree surgeon; cut your troubles off in the way dead branches are pruned from a tree.

If you are constantly naming your symptoms and discussing them, you give them power over you. You inhibit the kinetic action that releases the healing power and energy of your subconscious mind. By Law of Attraction, whatever you focus on or think about with emotion will expand and grow stronger.

A different kind of affirmation for the purpose of positive experiences throughout the day may be beneficial in the morning. For example, right after waking up, you could affirm out loud, "I am so grateful for this wonderful day. I will perform the required task today to the best of my ability, and I will experience only positive results. I will smile at everyone I meet and radiate only confidence and positive energy in my surroundings."

The latter affirmation is more appropriate when you are physically in a better state of mind. Different physical conditions require different treatments. In a later chapter, I will provide a more detailed guide on which reference to use on different conditions.

You were born with potential.
You were born with goodness and trust.
You were born with ideals and dreams.
You were born with greatness.
You were born with wings.
You are not meant for crawling, so don't.
You have wings.
Learn to use them and fly.

Rumi

*To defend one's self against
fear is simply to ensure that one
will one day be conquered by it;
fears must be faced.*

James Baldwin

Chapter 6

The Six Basic Fears

Fear always springs from ignorance.

Ralph Waldo Emerson

HERE ARE THE SIX BASIC FEARS from which every human suffers at one time or another, in the order that they most commonly appear:

- the fear of poverty

- the fear of criticism

- the fear of ill health

- the fear of loss of love of someone

- the fear of old age

- the fear of death

All other fears can be grouped under one of these six headings. Fears are nothing more than states of mind, and our state of mind is subject to control and direction. We humans have the ability to change our state of mind or redirect it through trusting our gut feelings and our education, or we can simply remove ourselves from an intensely negative energy field. These negative energy fields can be at your work place: a group of fellow employees worrying about the future of the company, or simply gossiping about the boss or the management. Gossiping of any kind, in the family, neighbourhood, or among friends, radiates very negative energy and must be avoided at any cost.

We have been given absolute control over only one thing, and that is thought. This fact, coupled with the fact that everything man creates begins in the form of a thought, leads us very close to the principle by which fear may be mastered. Because all thought has the tendency to clothe itself in its physical equivalent, it is equally true that negative thought impulses, like the fear of poverty or ill health, cannot be translated into courage, financial gain, or vibrant health.

You are what you think about

The fear of ill health is closely associated with the fear of old age and the fear of death. In general, humans are afraid of ill health because of the terrible pictures which have been planted in their minds of what may happen if death should overtake them. Research shows very convincingly that the fear of disease, even where there is not the slightest cause for fear, often produces the physical symptoms of the disease feared. Thus, campaigns of public awareness of certain diseases like Alzheimer's and cancer cause more harm than benefit.

Powerful and mighty is the human mind! It builds or it destroys

The Law of Attraction plays a major role in this scenario. Whatever you focus on or think about with emotion will expand.

When I was in the Army, many years ago, I was asked to speak in front of a group of fellow soldiers. I agreed to the request and didn't think of it again until I was standing in the spotlight in front of about 60 soldiers. I just froze, ran a blank, and left the stage deeply embarrassed, without saying anything.

In 2002, I joined Toastmasters International, an organization with clubs all over the world where members learn to overcome the fear of public speaking. In the process, other fears are eliminated as well, such as the fear of failure or the fear of success. Toastmasters can help you gain self confidence, learn leadership skills, and become a better person.

It's Up To Me

I get discouraged now and then
When there are clouds of gray,
Until I think about the things
That happened yesterday.
I do not mean the day before
Or those of month ago,
But all the yesterdays in which
I had the chance to grow.
I think of opportunities
That I allowed to die,
And those I took advantage of
Before they passed me by.
And I remember that the past
Presented quite a plight,
But somehow I endured it and
The future seemed all right.
And I remind myself that I
Am capable and free,
And my success and happiness
Are really up to me.

James J. Metcalfe

Chapter 7

How Your Subconscious Works While You Sleep

Your body believes every word you think and say
The healing system is the way the body mobilizes all
its resources to combat disease. The belief system
is often the activator of the healing system.

Norman Cousins

YOU AND I spend about one third of our life sleeping. This is an immutable fact of life. Sleep is a divine law, and many answers to our problems come to us when we are sound asleep.

Many people believe that we go to sleep to rest the body and that while we are sleeping a process to repair and rebuild our cells takes place. This is a gross misunderstanding. Nothing rests in sleep, except our conscious mind. Our heart, lungs, and all our vital organs function while we are asleep. If we eat before going to sleep, the food is digested and assimilated. Our skin secretes perspiration, and our hair and nails continue to grow.

Our subconscious mind never rests or sleeps. It is always active, controlling all our vital organs. The healing process takes place more rapidly while we are asleep because there is no interference from our conscious mind. Incredible answers to our daily problems are given to us while we are sleeping.

During the day, when we are awake, our conscious mind gets involved with distress, annoyance, and contentions. It needs to be able to withdraw periodically from our senses and the objective world and communicate silently with the inner wisdom of our subconscious mind. By seeking guidance, strength, and greater intelligence in all phases of our life, we will be able to overcome all or most difficulties.

This regular withdrawal from our conscious senses can be in the form of prayer, meditation, or just napping. Whatever takes us away from the noise and confusion of everyday living is also a form of sleep. That is, we become asleep to the world of our senses and alive to the wisdom and power of our subconscious mind.

Sleep deprivation can cause us to become irritable, moody, and depressed. All human beings need a minimum of eight hours of sleep to be healthy. Most people need more. Those who think they can get by on less sleep are fooling themselves. Medical research has established that sleep deprivation can cause severe mental and physical discomfort. Remember, we are spiritually recharged during sleep. Adequate sleep is essential for joy and vitality.

Our ability to solve problems creatively is most effective during sleep. Albert Einstein's theory of relativity came to him during sleep. Most of Thomas Edison's inventions came to him during sleep. I have solved many of my problems overnight, just by meditating before going to sleep and speaking out loud the following words: "The higher intelligence of my subconscious mind knows what is best for me, and it reveals to me the right decision, or the best solution. I feel blessed and I give thanks for the answer that I know will come to me."

I repeat this simple affirmation over and over as a lullaby until I drift off to sleep. Sometimes, during the night, the solution or answer appears in a dream. And sometimes I know the answer when I wake up in the morning.

Our subconscious mind is all-wise. It knows all things. Often it will speak to us, but in a voice our conscious mind will not accept. We may call it gut feeling or intuition, and we have to learn to trust it or have faith in it. Our intuition will never deceive us, but your conscious mind will.

To some, a warning may come in the form of a mother who appears in a dream. She tells the person not to go here or there, and gives her reason for the warning. Sometimes our subconscious will warn us in our waking hours. We think we hear a voice that sounds like our mother's voice or another loved one. We may stop and turn, looking for the source of the sound. Later we find that if we had continued on the way we were going, we might have been struck on the head by an object falling from a window.

Summary of your creative power while you sleep

1. If you have trouble waking up on time, suggest to your subconscious mind before sleep, the exact time you wish to wake up, and it will awaken you. It needs no clock. Do the same thing with all problems. There is nothing too hard for your subconscious.

2. Your subconscious never sleeps. It is always working on your vital functions. Forgive yourself and everyone else before you go to sleep, and healing will take place much more rapidly.

3. Guidance is given to you while you are asleep, sometimes in a dream. The healing energy is also released, and in the morning you feel refreshed and rejuvenated.

4. When troubled by the hectic activity and strife of the day, calm yourself down and think about the wisdom and intelligence lodged in your subconscious mind, which is ready to respond to you. This will give you peace, strength, and confidence.

5. Sleep is essential for peace of mind and health of body. Lack of sleep can cause irritation, depression, and mental disorders. You need eight hours of sleep every day.

6. You are spiritually recharged during sleep. Adequate sleep is essential for joy and vitality.

7. Your tired brain craves sleep so hungrily that it will sacrifice anything to get it. Many who have fallen asleep at the wheel of an automobile can testify to this.

8. Many sleep-deprived people have poor memories and lack proper coordination. They become confused and disoriented.
9. Sleep brings counsel. Before sleep, affirm that the infinite intelligence of your subconscious mind is guiding you. Then, watch for the solution that comes, perhaps in a dream or on awakening.
10. Trust your subconscious completely. Know that it will not deceive you. Sometimes, your subconscious answers you in a very vivid dream and a vision in the night.
11. Your future is in your mind now, based on your habitual thinking and beliefs. Believe that your subconscious will lead and guide you, and understand that all good is yours. If you do, your future will be wonderful. Believe it and accept it. Expect the best, and the best will come to you.
12. If you are writing a novel, a play, a song, or a poem, or working on an invention, speak to your subconscious mind at night. Claim boldly that its wisdom, intelligence, and power are revealing the ideal plot, melody, or rhyme, or that it is revealing the perfect solution, whatever it may be. Miracles will happen as you pray this way.

You will see it when you believe it

Chapter 8

The Power of Visualization

You see things; and you say, "Why?"
But I dream things that never were;
and I say, "Why not?"

George Bernard Shaw

MOST PEOPLE LIVE AND DIE and never fully understand the power of imagination. We need to understand and appreciate that the ability to visualize comes from the imagination. And visualization is the key to a healthy life.

Whatever you can perceive and believe, you can achieve. Although I am relating this idea to "health" in this book, I want you to know that once you fully understand the concept of visualization, you can effectively use it for whatever good you desire. Be it wealth, prosperity, relationships, the ideal partner, the ideal job, the ideal residence – whatever you can imagine is possible, you can achieve.

Every human being has always used the concept of visualization. In fact, everything that has ever come into our life has come as a direct result of the visualization process. If we become aware of the results we have produced, we will realize we have already employed this great mental tool. Just take a look at other people's results: it is quite obvious that they almost always use visualization the wrong way.

"Images" are mental pictures made from thoughts, and the magnificence of the mind lies in the fact that it can "think." It can tap into thought and create whatever image it chooses.

Play with your mind for a few minutes and become aware of how you can flash one picture or image after another on the screen of your mind. It is almost as if you were sitting in a great theatre, and you are the writer, producer, and director of the movie you are watching.

In his book, *You Were Born Rich*, Bob Proctor talks about visualization in a chapter called "The Image Maker" The ideas in this chapter are so powerful, that I would recommend reading it a few times.

Commitment

There is one elementary truth,
The ignorance of which kills
countless ideas and splendid plans:
that the moment one definitely
commits oneself,
then providence moves too.
All sorts of things occur to help one
that would never otherwise have occurred.
A whole stream of events
issues from the decision
raising in one's favour all manner of
unforeseen incidents and meetings and
material assistance
which no one could have dreamed
would have come their way.
Whatever you can do or dream you can, begin it.
Boldness has genius, power, and magic in it.
Begin it now.

Johann Wolfgang von Goethe

Chapter 9

The Law of Attraction

As he thinketh in his heart, so is he.

Proverbs 23:7

IF YOU CONSTANTLY VISUALIZE a negative or frightening image in your mind based on a negative memory of your past *that* is what you will produce in your life. The Law of Attraction is always working. You get what you think about, whether you want it or not.

The powerful Law of Attraction draws to you whatever you are predominantly thinking about. So if you think about the things you desire, your life experience will reflect those things. And, in the same way, if you are predominantly thinking about what you do not want, your life experience reflects those more negative things.

A random thought doesn't have much attraction power because it is not strong enough to become manifested into reality. But when you add emotion to your thoughts, the attraction power becomes stronger in direct relation to your emotion. Whenever you are thinking about something with emotion, you are essentially planning your future. When you are appreciating something, you are planning. When you are worrying, you are planning. However, worrying is using your imagination to create something you do not really want, while happiness and appreciation create a better future.

How does this work? Basically, every thought, every idea, every being, every thing is vibration. When you focus your attention on something, even for a short period of time, the vibration of your Being begins to reflect the vibration of that to which you are giving your attention. The more you think about it, the more you vibrate like it; the more you vibrate like it, the more likely it is that other things like it will also be attracted to you. In other words, things that match that vibration are drawn to you, by you.

When you understand the Law of Attraction, you are never surprised by what occurs in your life, because you understand that you have invited every bit of it through your own thought and visualization process. Nothing can occur in your life experience without your invitation.

Because there are no exceptions to the powerful Law of Attraction, a thorough understanding of it is easy to achieve. And once you understand that you get what you think about, and equally as important, when you are aware of what you are thinking, then you are in a position to exercise absolute control of your own experience.

If there is something you desire that you currently do not have, you need only turn your full attention to it, and by the Law of Attraction, it will come to you.

However, if there is something you desire that you currently do not have and you pay attention to your current state of *not* having it, then the Law of Attraction will continue to match that "not-having-it-vibration," so you will continue to not have that which you desire.

The key to bringing into your experience what you desire is to achieve vibration harmony with what you desire. The easiest way to do this is to pretend that it is already in your reality. Guide your thoughts toward the enjoyment of that experience, and as you practice these thoughts and begin to consistently offer that vibration, you will be allowing it into your life.

We humans have a built-in internal guidance system that tells us how we feel about our thoughts. You can easily know if you are giving full attention to your desire, or if you are paying more attention to the absence of your desire. When the vibration of your thoughts match your desire, you feel good; your emotional range will be from contentment to expectation to eagerness to joy. Conversely, if you are giving your attention to the lack or absence of your desire, your emotions will range from feelings of pessimism to worry to anger to insecurity to depression.

As you become consciously aware of your emotions, you will never again misunderstand why things are turning out the way they are. Your emotions provide a wonderful guidance system for you. And if you pay attention to them, you can guide yourself to anything that you desire.

Here are some examples you might be able to relate to. There is a big difference in the vibration frequency in your thoughts about your appreciation of your mate versus the thoughts of what you'd like to be different in your mate. The relationship with your partner reflects the dominate thoughts you have about this relationship. You may not have done it consciously, but you have literally thought your relationship into being.

Your desire for an improved health condition cannot come to you if you feel jealous of your friend's healthy condition, because the vibration of your desire and the vibration of your jealous feeling are at very different frequencies.

An understanding of your vibration nature will make it possible for you to deliberately create your own reality. And in time and with practice, you will discover that all desire you hold can be realized – for there is nothing that you cannot be, do, or have.

Even though it may seem odd to you at first, it will be helpful to you to accept yourself as a vibrant being, because it is a vibrant universe in which you are living. The laws that govern this universe are based on vibration frequencies.

Once you become consciously aware of the universal laws, and gain an understanding of why things respond the way they do, mystery and confusion will be replaced by clarity and understanding. Doubt and fear will be replaced with knowledge and confidence – and joy will become the basic premise of your experience.

There are no complicated courses for you to study in preparation for understanding the information presented here. I am writing this book so that you can begin to receive value from right where you are. You are ready for this information, right now, and this information is ready for you. For more on this subject, see *"Ask and it is Given"* by Esther and Jerry Hicks.

Chapter 10

The Power of Intention

Every moment of your life is infinitely creative,
and the universe is endlessly bountiful.
Just put forward a clear enough request,
and everything your heart desires
must come to you.

Shakti Gawain

EVERY PERSON ON THIS PLANET has the potential to be a healer. But in order to experience your inherent healing powers, you must first make the decision to be healed yourself. Once you've accepted your power to heal yourself and optimize your health, you become someone who's capable of healing others as well.

In *The Power of Intention*, Dr. Wayne W. Dyer explains very convincingly how all human beings are connected to a Higher Intelligence or, as he calls it, Source Energy. That Source is never focused on what's wrong, or what's missing. True healing takes you back to the Source. If you don't believe that you are connected to this higher intelligence, then you have created resistance to your intention to heal and be healed. If you believe that it is possible, but not for you, then you have more resistance. If you believe you are being punished by the absence of health, that's also resistance. These thoughts about your ability to be healed play a dominant role in your physical health. Research shows that healing through intention, which is actually healing through connecting to the Higher Intelligence or Source, is possible for everyone. But it means letting go of the fear that permeates your consciousness. And it also means recognizing the fear-based energy promoted by the health care industry.

Any disease process is evidence that something is amiss. Any fear associated with the disease process is further evidence that the mind is misperceiving something. Health and peace are the natural state when that which prevents them is removed, meaning fear and other misperceptions.

But how do you do this? First, become aware of the thoughts you have that support the idea of sickness as something to be expected. Become aware of how often you have those thoughts. The more they occupy your mind, the more resistance you create to prevent healing.

You are likely familiar with the following typical thoughts of resistance. You may even have used them yourself:

- I can't do anything about this arthritis.
- It's the flu season.
- I feel okay now, but by the weekend, it will be in my chest and I'll have fever.
- Everything is either fattening or filled with chemicals.
- I feel so tired all the time.

You need to understand that these thoughts and others like them are blocking the realization of your intention. They show that you are buying into the illness mentality of huge profit-making drug companies and a health care industry that thrives on your fears.

However, you don't have to think this way. You can choose to think that you have the ability to raise your energy level, even if all the advertising around you points to a different conclusion. Go within yourself and say:

"I want to feel good, I intend to feel good, I intend to return to my Source, and I refuse to allow any thoughts of *dis-order* or *dis-ease* in."

You will feel empowered by these affirmations. In any given moment when you are not feeling well, choose thoughts of healing and feeling good. At that moment, feeling good takes over, if only for a few seconds.

When you choose to live in high energy, and you work moment by moment to introduce thoughts that support your intention, you've effectively decided that wellness is your choice and that being healed is part of that decision. At this point everything you desire or need to fulfill your personal intention will appear. How can that be? In the quote from Goethe, one of the most brilliant scholars and achievers in the history of humanity gives you the answer. The moment you definitely commit yourself to being a part of the power of intention, "then providence moves too," and unforeseen assistance comes your way.

The right people will come into your life to assist you in every aspect of your life: people who will support you in your career, people who will arrange the finances for whatever you desire, and your spiritual soul mate finds you.

The list is endless, because we're all in relationship to each other, we all come from the same Source, and we all share the same divine energy. There is no place that this universal energy is not; therefore, you share it with everyone you attract into your life.

You have to let go of any resistance to your ability to attract the right people, or you won't recognize them when they show up in your life. Resistance may be difficult to recognize at first, because it is such a familiar form of your thoughts and your emotions. If you believe that you're powerless to attract the right people, then you have attracted powerlessness into your life. If you think of being stuck with the wrong people or no people at all, then your energy isn't aligned with the power of intention, and resistance reigns. The universal energy has no choice but to send you more of what you desire. You have to make a leap into the inconceivable, where you have faith. Trust in the universal mind of intention and allow the right people to arrive into your life space right on schedule.

The universal all-creating energy is already cooperating with your intention, more by default then by purposeful creation. The people you seek are obviously already here, and you also share the same divine Source of all life with them, since everyone comes from that Source. In some invisible way, you're already connected spiritually to those perfect-for-you people. Why can't you see them, touch them, or hold them? And why aren't they with you when you need them?

The right people will show up and appear to you only when you are ready and willing to receive them. They've always been there. They're there right now. They'll always be there. The questions you have to ask yourself are:

- Am I ready?
- Am I willing?
- How much am I willing to have it?

If your answers to these questions are a readiness and willingness to experience your desires, then you will begin seeing people and events entering your life on these levels and you will recognize them immediately.

Once you've formed a picture in your mind of the person or the event that you intend to show up in your life, and you know how you want to be treated and what it will be like, you must *be* what it is you are seeking. This is a universe of attraction and energy. You can't have a desire to attract a mate who's confident, generous, nonjudgmental, and gentle, and expect that desire to be manifested if you are thinking and acting in non-confident, selfish, judgmental, or arrogant ways – which is why most people don't attract the right people at the right time. For more on this subject, see Dr. Wayne W. Dyer's *The Power of Intention*.

MY CREED

To live as gently as I can;
To be, no matter where, a man;
To take what comes of good or ill
And cling to faith and honor still;
To do my best, and let that stand
The record of my brain and hand;
And then, should failure come to me,
Still work and hope for victory.
To have no secret place wherein
I stop unseen to shame or sin;
To be the same when I'm alone
As when my every deed is known;
To live undaunted, unafraid
Of any step that I have made;
To be without pretense or sham
Exactly what men think I am.
This, I believe, is all I need
For my philosophy and creed.

Edgar A. Guest

Chapter 11

Thinking in a Special Way

*The service we render to others is
really the rent we pay for our
room on this earth. It is obvious that
man is himself a traveler; that
the purpose of this world is not
"to have and to hold" but "to give
and serve." There can be no other meaning.*

Sir Wilfred T. Grenfell

WHEN YOU FIND YOURSELF in a group of people like in a workshop, a seminar or a presentation where you don't have much time to get to know each other, and a situation arises where you have to find a leader in a small group, it will be apparent very quickly who is likely to become the leader in that group. The person with the strongest leadership qualities and charisma will most likely get the position, because that person is thinking in a special way.

This chapter is inspired by Wallace D. Wattles' *The Science of Getting Rich*. To attain wealth and good health requires pretty much the same thought process and physical activity: that's why I decided to include his wisdom.

If you work hard during the course of your career, and you reach the career level in your life to a certain level of accomplishment, for example; middle management, that position is yours, you own it, and nobody can take it away from you. If you change companies during the course of your career, you never have to start at the bottom again. That position will be yours again and an even higher position could be yours on the ladder you are climbing. Again, this happens if you think in a special way.

We are living in a world of abundance. There is enough room and space on this planet for all living creatures to live comfortably. We have enough air to breathe, water to drink, food to eat, and enough natural resources to clothe ourselves and build shelter. All our necessities for a comfortable life are already taken care of. In this world of abundance, we don't need to be modest, and we have permission to ask for what we want without infringing on the rights of others.

This is a difficult point with most people. They may think that poverty and sacrifice are pleasing to God. They look at poverty as a part of the plan, as a necessity of nature, considering that the majority of humanity must stay poor because there is not enough to go around. People who hold to this erroneous thought are ashamed to ask for wealth. They try to want just enough to be fairly comfortable. The same thing holds true for health. Many people think that their suffering is a normal part of life – they are ashamed to want more. *Neither poverty nor ill health is a necessity of nature.*

I want to tell you about a student who was told that he must see in his mind a clear picture of the things he desired so that the creative thought of them might be impressed upon a formless substance. He was a very poor man, living in a rented house, and having only what he earned from day to day. He could not imagine the fact that all wealth was his. After thinking the matter over, he decided that he might reasonably ask for a new rug for the floor of his best room and an oscillating fan to keep him cool on the hot summer days. After following the instructions given in his book, he obtained these things in a few weeks. Then it dawned upon him that he had not asked enough. He went through the house in which he lived and planned all the improvements he would like to make in it. He mentally added a fireplace here and a bay window there and a laundry room somewhere else. He continued until it was complete in his mind as his ideal home. After that, he planned its furnishings.

Writing down his plans and goals, and holding the whole picture in his mind, he began thinking in that special way and moving toward his goals and dreams. He now owns the house, and is rebuilding it according to his mental image. Now with still larger faith, he is accomplishing greater things. It has been done unto him according to his faith, and it is so with you and with all of us.

Like this man, you must form a clear and definite mental picture of what you want. You cannot transmit an idea to the universal energy unless you have it in your mind first. You must have it before you can give it. Many people have only a vague and cloudy concept of the things they want to do, to have, or to become. It is not enough that you have a general desire to be healthy or "to do well with." Most people have that desire. It is not enough that you have a wish to travel, see things, live better, etc. Most people have those desires as well.

If you want to send a text message to a friend, you would not take words at random from the dictionary. You would send a coherent sentence; one which meant something. When you send out prayers, wishes, and desires, it must be done with a coherent statement. You must know what you want, and be definite. You can never get your desires fulfilled or start creative power into action by sending out unformed longings and vague desires.

Go over your desires, just as the man I have described went over his house. See what you want and get a clear mental picture of what you want it to look like when you get it. Visualize it. As the sailor has the port towards which he is sailing fixed in his mind, you must have a clear mental picture continually in your mind. You must not lose sight of it, any more than the steersman can lose sight of the compass.

Spend as much of your leisure time as you can in contemplating your picture. Keep in mind that no one needs to take exercises to concentrate his or her mind on a thing which he or she really wants. It is the things you do not really care about which require effort.

Unless your desire to get healthy is strong enough to hold your thoughts to the purpose — as the magnetic pole holds the needle of the compass — it will hardly be worthwhile for you to carry out the instructions given in this book. The methods presented here are for people whose desire to become healthy is strong enough to overcome mental laziness and taking the easy way out.

The more clear and definite you make your picture, and the more you dwell upon it, the stronger your desire will be. And the stronger your desire, the easier it will be to think about the picture of what you want.

Behind your clear vision must be the purpose to realize it, to bring it out in reality. And behind this purpose must be an invincible and unshakable faith that you have the power within you to overcome any discomfort, disease or physical weakness.

"Whatsoever things ye ask for when ye pray, believe that ye receive them, and you shall have them," said Jesus.

You do not need to pray repeatedly for the things you want. Your higher intelligence knows what you need and what is good for you. Your part is to intelligently formulate your desire for the things that make a larger life and to get these desires arranged into a coherent whole. You must then impress this whole desire upon the formless substance, which has the power and the will to bring you what you want. You do not make this impression by repeating strings of words. Rather, you make it by holding the vision with unshakable purpose to attain it — and with steadfast faith that you will attain it.

Once you have clearly formed your vision, the whole matter turns to receiving. From that moment on, you must receive in your mind what you ask for. Think and speak of all the things you have asked for in terms of actual present reality. Imagine the exact environment and condition you desire and live all the time in that imaginary environment and condition. Be aware that you do not do this as a mere dreamer and castle builder. Remember that it is faith and purpose in the use of imagination which make the difference between the scientist and the dreamer. And having learned this fact, you must now learn the proper use of the will.

You do not try to apply your willpower to anything outside of yourself. You have no right to do so anyway. It is wrong to apply your will to other men and women in order to get them to do what you wish done.

It is absolutely wrong to coerce people by mental power, just as it is to coerce them by physical power. If compelling people by physical force to do things for you reduces them to slavery, compelling them by mental means is exactly the same thing. The only difference is in the methods. If taking things from people by physical force is robbery, then taking things by mental force is also robbery. In principle there is no difference. Clever salespersons using hard-sell methods come to mind. You have no right to use your will power upon another person – even "for his or her own good" – because you do not know what is good for him or her.

You do not have to compel God to give you good things, any more than you have to use your will power to make the sun rise. The thinking substance is friendly to you and is more anxious to give you what you want than you are to get it. You need only to use your will power upon yourself.

When you know what to think and do, you must use your will to compel yourself to think and do the right things. That is the legitimate use of the will in getting what you want. Use your will to keep yourself thinking and acting in that special way.

Do not try to project your will or your thoughts or your mind out into space to act on things or people. Keep your mind at home, where it can accomplish more than elsewhere.

Use your mind to form a mental image of what you want and to hold that vision with faith and purpose. Use your will to keep your mind working the right way.

The more steady and continuous your faith and purpose, the faster you will heal, because you will make only positive impressions upon your higher intelligence. The higher intelligence receives a picture of your desires and allows this picture to penetrate great distances – perhaps throughout the entire universe.

As this impression spreads, all things are set in motion toward its realization. All force begins to be exerted in that direction. All things begin to move toward you. The minds of people everywhere are influenced toward doing the things necessary to fulfilling your desires. And they work for you unconsciously.

You can check all this by sending a negative impression toward your higher intelligence. Doubt or disbelief is as certain to start a movement away from you as faith and purpose are to start one toward you. By not understanding this, most people fail when they try to make use of "mental science."

Every moment you spend in giving energy to doubts and fears, every moment you spend in worry, every moment in which your soul is possessed by disbelief sends a current away from you through the entire domain of the higher intelligence.

"All the promises are unto them that believe and unto them only." Notice how insistent Jesus was upon this point of belief. Now you know the reason why.

As your beliefs are shaped to a very great extent by the things you observe and think about, it is important that you focus your attention. Now your *will* comes into use, because by means of your will, you determine the objects of your attention.

Health is never attained by studying disease and thinking about disease. Things are not brought into being by thinking about their opposites. Righteousness is not to be promoted by studying sin and thinking about sin. If you want to become rich, you must not make a study of poverty.

Medicine as a science of disease has increased disease. Religion as a science of sin has promoted sin. And economics as a study of poverty will fill the world with unhappiness, misery, deficiency, and need.

Do not talk about your illness or any other illness again to anyone, except your doctor or healthcare practitioner. Do not talk about poverty. Do not investigate it or concern yourself with it. It is unimportant what its causes are. What concerns you is the cure.

You cannot hold the mental image which is necessary to make you well if you fill your mind with pictures of illness, disease, poverty, and crime. You need to have pictures of healthy people in your mind. Do not watch TV programs about hospitals, emergency rooms, surgery, and medical treatments.

The widespread knowledge of symptoms, diseases, and medical treatments does not eliminate illnesses and physical ailments. Illness can be done away with only by increasing the number of sick people who succeed in getting well through the exercise of faith, purpose, and a sense of responsibility for the condition they are in. People must be taught to get healthy by their own merits, not by chemicals.

Everything said so far applies only to illnesses and diseases. *It does <u>not</u> apply to accident victims or personal injury.* If you are in a car accident with a ruptured liver or kidney, you better get to the nearest hospital emergency room and have a medical professional take care of you.

Too Strong For Fear

Promise yourself to be so strong that nothing can disturb your peace of mind.

To talk health, happiness and prosperity to every person you meet. To make all your friends feel that there is something in them.

To look at the sunny side of everything and make your optimism come true.

To think only of the best, to work only for the best and expect only the best. To be just as enthusiastic about the success of others as you are about your own.

To forget the mistakes of the past and press on to the greater achievements of the future.

To wear a cheerful countenance at all times and give every living creature you meet a smile.

To give so much time to the improvement of yourself that you have no time to criticize others.

To be too large for worry, too noble for anger, too strong for fear and too happy to permit the presence of trouble.

Christian D. Larson

Chapter 12

Fear – Our Strongest Opponent

The only thing we have to fear is fear itself.

F. D. Roosevelt – Inaugural Address, 1933

WHEN I WAS about three years old, I was with my whole family, my parents and my two older sisters on an island in the northern part of Germany. It was our annual family vacation. We went to the beach every day, and I enjoyed playing in the sand, digging holes, baking imaginary cakes and cookies. My castle-building ability wasn't developed at that time, but I remember having great fun playing in the sand. Subconsciously I knew there was water somewhere nearby, but as long as I couldn't see it and was far enough away from it, I didn't care. One day my mother took me in her arms and carried me towards the water.

When I realized what was happening, I indicated to her that I didn't like it and didn't want to go there. She calmed me down by saying that I was safe in her arms. When we came closer to the water, I started crying and tried to get down. She kept walking closer to the water, holding me firm in an attempt to help me overcome my fear of water. When I saw the water touching her feet, all hell broke loose within me. My loud screaming and pushing finally convinced her that this was not helping me at all. She tried a few more times, but to no avail.

When I was six or seven years old, my parents told me during a family conversation that I already had this abnormal fear of water when I was only a year old. But at the age of ten, I learned how to swim in a local swimming pool during a school program, in a few weeks. I later swam in the ocean without fear while in a Boy Scout program.

Fast forward 40 years: I participated in a special meditation class to regress back to birth. During the meditation I recalled a conversation between my older sisters when I was about two or three weeks of age. I overheard my four-year-old sister talking to my two-year-old sister: "You know there is big water called 'Ocean.' This is very dangerous, you can drown in it and than you die." I guess I decided right then and there that the big water was no good for me, and my childhood fear of ocean water was established.

A newborn baby has only two basic fears: the fear of sudden loud noise and the fear of falling. These fears serve as a sort of alarm system given to you by nature for self-preservation.

Normal fear is good. When you hear a car coming down the road towards you, and you step aside to survive, the fear of being run over is overcome by your action. All other fears are learned or were acquired later on in life by particular experiences or were passed along to you by parents, relatives, teachers, and others who influenced you.

Many students suffer from the fear of failure, or what we call "suggestive amnesia" during examinations. They know the material cold before the exam and remember all the answers after the exam. But when in the classroom, they stare down at an exam booklet with a totally blank mind.

Here is a technique for overcoming fear that I learned from Dr. Joseph Murphy's book, *The Power of your Subconscious Mind*. It works well with many fears and is very effective.

If you are afraid of swimming, make time to sit still for about ten minutes three or four times a day. Put yourself into a state of deep relaxation, as I have explained earlier in the book. Now imagine you are swimming. Subjectively, you are swimming. Mentally, you have placed yourself into the water. You feel the brisk coolness of the water and the movement of your arms and legs. It is all real, vivid, and a joyous activity of the mind.

This is not idle daydreaming. Your subconscious mind can't tell the difference between imagined and real experiences. Understand that what you are experiencing in your imagination will be developed in your subconscious mind. Then you will be compelled to express the image and likeness of the picture you impressed on your deeper mind. When you next attempt to swim, it is the joy that will surface. This is the law of the subconscious.

If you find yourself overwhelmed with an abnormal fear, you must strive to move mentally to the opposite extreme. As long as you remain at the extreme of fear, you will suffer stagnation plus mental and physical deterioration. When fear arises, usually the subconscious mind brings with it a desire for something opposite what you fear. So concentrate immediately on the thing desired, not on the fear. Get absorbed and engrossed in your desire.

Understand that the subjective always overturns the objective. This attitude will give you confidence and lift your spirits. The infinite power of your subconscious mind is moving on your behalf. It cannot fail. Therefore, peace and comfort are yours.

Ralph Waldo Emerson, the great philosopher and poet said, Do the thing you are afraid to do, and the death of fear is certain.

If I had not joined Toastmasters International to overcome my fear of public speaking, I would never have been able to share with others what I have learned about physical health. And I am sure you would not be reading this book.

STEPS TO FREEDOM FROM FEAR

1. Do the things you are afraid to do, and the death of fear is certain. If you say to yourself with perfect confidence and faith, "I am going to master this fear," you will master it.

2. Fear is humanity's greatest enemy. It is behind failure, sickness, and bad human relations. Love casts out fear. Love is an emotional attachment to the good things of life. Fall in love with honesty, integrity, justice, goodwill, and success. Expect the best in your life, and invariably, the best will come to you.

3. Fear is behind the suggestive amnesia that strikes during examinations. You can overcome this by affirming frequently, "I have a perfect memory for everything I need to know." Imagine a friend congratulating you on your brilliant success on your exam.

4. If you are afraid of closed places, such as elevators, mentally ride in an elevator while sincerely blessing all its parts and functions. You will be amazed how quickly the fear will disappear.

5. You were born with only two fears, the fear of falling and the fear of loud noise. All your other fears were acquired. Get rid of them.

6. Normal fear is good. Abnormal fear is destructive. To constantly indulge in thoughts of fear will result in abnormal fears, obsessions, and complexes. To fear something persistently causes a sense of panic and terror.

7. You can overcome abnormal fear when you know the power of your subconscious mind, which can change conditions and can manifest the desires of your heart. Give your immediate attention and devotion to your desire, which is the opposite of your fear. This is the love that casts out fear.

8. If you are afraid of failure, give attention to success. If you are afraid of sickness, dwell on perfect health. If you are afraid of an accident, dwell on the guidance and protection of God and work on overcoming your feeling of guilt.

9. The great law of substitution is the answer to fear. Whatever you fear has its solution in the form of your desire. If you are sick, you desire health. If you are in the prison of fear, you desire freedom. Mentally concentrate on the good, and know that your subconscious mind always answers you. It never fails.

10. The things you fear do not really exist except as thoughts in your mind. But thoughts are creative. So look at your fears; hold them up to the light of reason. Learn to laugh at yourself. That is the best medicine. Nothing can disturb you but your own thoughts. The suggestions, statements, or threats of other persons have no power. The power is within you, and when your thoughts are focused on that which is good, God's power is with your thoughts of good.

Lord, make me an instrument of Your Peace.

Where there is hatred, let me sow love;

Where there is injury, pardon;

Where there is doubt, faith;

Where there is despair, hope;

Where there is darkness, light;

And where there is sadness, joy.

O Divine Master, grant that I may not so much seek

To be consoled as to console;

To be understood as to understand;

To be loved as to love;

For it is in giving that we receive;

It is in pardoning that we are pardoned;

And it is in dying that we are born to eternal light.

St. Francis of Assisi

Chapter 13

Love Conquers All

Love and life are inseparable from each other.
Where there is life, there is love.
Even on the most rudimentary
level of consciousness,
living things reach beyond their
limitations and merge
with other forms…It is the cosmic glue
that holds the universe together.

Douglas Bloch

CAN YOU REMEMBER the last time you were in love? Your heart went "Ahhh." It was such a wonderful feeling! It is the same thing with loving yourself, except that you will never leave. Once you have your love for yourself, it is with you for the rest of your life, and you want to make it the best relationship you can have.

As adults, we cannot expect to be loved by anyone more than we are able to love ourselves. What we think about us becomes the truth for us. I believe that everyone, myself included, is 100 percent responsible for the experiences in our lives, the best and the worst. Every thought we think, is creating our future.

The thoughts we think and the words we speak determine our actions, and our actions consequently create our experiences.

We create our situations, and we give our power away if we blame another person for our frustration. In fact, no other person, place, or thing has any power over us because "we" are the only thinkers in our mind. We create our experiences, our reality, and everyone in that reality. When we create peace and harmony and balance in our minds, we will find it in our lives.

I believe that everything in this universe is energy; manifested and non-manifested energy, which vibrates on different frequencies. I also believe that our body, mind, and soul work on different frequency levels as one unit, fulfilling our purpose while we are here.

Every one of us decided to incarnate on this planet at a particular time and in a specific space. We have chosen to come here to learn a particular lesson that will advance us on our spiritual pathway. We chose our sex, our colour, our country, and the particular set of parents who teach us the lessons we need to learn in this lifetime. When we grow up, many of us blame our parents for the troubles we find ourselves in. But in reality, we chose them because they were perfect for what we came here to learn.

We learn our belief systems very early in life, and we move through life creating experiences that match our beliefs. Notice in your own life how often you have gone though the same or a similar experience. I believe you created those experiences over and over because they mirrored something you believe about yourself.

All the events you have experienced in your lifetime up to this point have been created by the thoughts, words, and actions you used yesterday, last week, last month, last year, or many years ago, depending on how old you are. However, that is your past. It is over and done with. What is important in this moment is what you are choosing to think and believe and say and do right now. For these thoughts, words, and actions will create your future. Your point of power is at the present moment and is forming the experiences of tomorrow, next week, next month, next year, and into the future.

When you have a problem, regardless of what the problem is, your experiences are just an outer reflection of your inner thoughts. Even self-hatred really only hates a thought you have about yourself. You have a thought that says, "I am a bad person." This thought produces a feeling, and you buy into the feeling. Remember, feelings and emotions are the power of creation, and in this case, it is self-punishment. This is the way accidents happen. I personally don't believe in accidents, and look at them rather as subconsciously created self-punishment. Who in his or her right mind would admit openly to inflicting damage or injuring him/herself? It is so much easier to blame it on an accident.

If two separate people are involved in a car accident, I call it a subconscious co-creation of one event: two different drivers who are vibrating at a similar frequency level attract each other like a magnet. Even though traffic regulations draw a different picture, the so-called innocent victim co-created the event on a subconscious level.

The reality is that most of us were brought up with the belief that when we made a mistake our parents would punish us. When we grow into adulthood, nobody is there to punish us for our mistakes anymore. But because we are still making mistakes, our feelings of guilt and shame dictate to us the appropriate level of punishment. People with strong feelings of guilt and shame can create a number of accidents. People who hardly ever feel guilty or ashamed seldom or never have accidents.

Let us not use this information as an excuse to stay stuck in our fear and discomfort, however. The past has no power over us. It doesn't matter how long we have had a negative pattern. The point of power is in the present moment. What a wonderful thing to realize! We can begin to be free in this moment.

We may habitually think the same thought over and over, so often, in fact, that it doesn't seem we are choosing the thought. But we did make the original choice. We can refuse to think certain thoughts. Look at how often you have refused to think a positive thought about yourself. You can also refuse to think a negative thought about yourself. I believe that everyone on this planet is suffering from self-hatred and guilt to one degree or another. The more self-hatred and guilt we have, the less our lives are working. The less self-hatred and guilt we have, the better our lives work.

I find that resentment, criticism, guilt, and fear cause more problems in our lives than anything else. These feelings come from blaming others and not taking responsibility for our own experiences. If we are all 100 percent responsible for everything in our lives, then there is no one to blame. Whatever is happening "out there" is only a mirror of our own internal thinking. I am not condoning other people's poor behaviour, but it is *our beliefs* that attract the people who treat us badly.

If you find yourself saying things like, "Everyone always criticizes me, no one is ever there for me, he/she uses me like a door mat, he/she abuses me," then this is *your pattern.* There is some thought in you that attracts people who exhibit this behaviour towards you. When you no longer think this way, they will go elsewhere and do it to somebody else. You will no longer attract them.

These negative thinking patterns not only create experiences outside of us, but they also affect us inside our physical bodies. All physical ailments or symptoms can be traced back to a corresponding thinking pattern. I want to mention a few samples out of my own life.

Cancer is an illness of resentment. I resented my childhood and many other things of my past, which I should have left behind long ago. Because I carried that resentment into adulthood, I created colon cancer. The colon represents our ability to let go, to release that which we no longer need. The liver represents the seat of primitive emotion. Because I was a very angry person in my youth, I created liver cancer. An anger management class helped me to eliminate it. My chronic bronchitis was caused by my fear of life. My lower back pain was caused by material worries. My angina pectoris was caused by the lack of joy in my life.

I obtained this information from Louise L. Hay's book, *You Can Heal Your Life.* Hay is a cancer survivor as well, and she did extensive research on the link between thought patterns and physical symptoms. Her little blue book, *Heal Your Body*, became my Bible many years ago, and I know it by heart. If you want to know the mental thought pattern that is causing your own physical symptoms, *Heal Your Body* is a must-have.

Hay's books teach you how to love yourself. You have to be able to love yourself first, before anyone else can feel love for you. I found the following in one of her books, and I want to pass it on to you:

The Golden Gate

There is no difficulty that enough love will not conquer.
There is no disease that enough love will not heal.
No door that enough love will not open.
No gulf that enough love will not bridge.
No wall that enough love will not throw down.
And no sin that enough love will not redeem.
It makes no difference how deeply seated may be the trouble.
How hopeless the outlook. How muddled the tangle.
How great the mistake.
A sufficient realization of love will dissolve it all.
And if you could love enough you would be the happiest
and most powerful person in the world.

Emmet Fox

This sounds wonderful, and it is true.

What do *you* need to do to get to that space where you could be the happiest and the most powerful person in the world?

We are just beginning to learn about the power we have inside. We are not going to find it if we close ourselves down. The more we can open up to ourselves and to others, the more likely we are to find the universal energies available to assist us. We are capable of incredible accomplishments.

The following experience I had with my good friend Lydia is a powerful example of what is possible.

On a warm autumn weekend, we were working in the back yard doing some gardening. As a refreshment, we were sharing an open pop can. Lydia took a drink from the pop can, not realizing that a wasp was inside the can. The wasp entered her mouth and stung her on the back of her tongue. She immediately had breathing problems and couldn't talk. I offered to take her to emergency, but she declined, indicating that I should help her get to the bedroom so she could lie down and make contact with her higher power. She gave me a sign to leave the room. I reluctantly left; I was aware that people have died with similar stings because they didn't get emergency treatment quickly enough.

I opened the door quietly and peeked into the room to see if Lydia was all right. She was lying on her side, lost in prayer. I did this every minute for about 10 minutes, before going downstairs to wait in the living room. After half an hour, she came down to the living room, visibly exhausted. She had some pain in her throat but was otherwise fine. To me, this miracle clearly shows the power of human potential.

You too can experience the miracle of the human potential. Take a few breaths. Open your chest and give your heart room to expand. Keep practicing, and sooner or later, the barriers will come down. Today is your beginning point.

For more on this subject, see *You Can Heal Your Life, by* Louise Hay.

Decide to Forgive

Decide to forgive
For resentment is negative
Resentment is poisonous
Resentment diminishes
and devours the self.
Be the first to forgive,
To smile and to take the first step,
And you will see happiness bloom
On the face of your human
brother or sister.
Be always the first
Do not wait for others to forgive.

The Power of Forgiveness

To err is human, to forgive, divine.

Pope — Essay on Criticism

FORGIVENESS OF OTHERS is necessary to attain mental peace and vibrant health. You must forgive everyone who has ever hurt you in the past, if you want good health and happiness in your life.

By the same token, you must also forgive yourself for all the wrongs you have ever done in your life. That doesn't mean that you have to condone all the wrongs done unto you in your life or condone the mistakes you have made. It simply means that you are willing to stop judging them.

The strange thing with forgiveness is that it is impossible to forgive yourself completely until you have forgiven everyone else first. So, start by forgiving others first. It doesn't matter if those people are alive or not, in your presence or not, because you are not taking the burden of guilt off their shoulders. You are relieving yourself of the burden of resentment, hate, anger, and blame. You are the only one who will benefit from the process.

In the field of psychosomatic medicine, it is emphasized that resentment, condemnation of others, and hostility are behind a number of medical problems, ranging from arthritis to lung and cardiac disease. The stress caused by these negative emotions can directly affect the immune system of the body, leaving you open to infection and disease.

Specialists in stress-related disorders point out that people who are mistreated, deceived, or injured often react with resentment and hatred towards those who hurt them. This reaction causes inflamed and festering wounds in their subconscious minds. The best remedy for this is to cut out and discard their hurts, and the only sure way to do this is by forgiveness.

The most important part of forgiving another person is the willingness to forgive. Lip service is not enough; it has to come from your heart. If you sincerely desire to forgive the other person, you are more than halfway over the hurdle.

Keep in mind that to forgive someone does not mean that you have to like or associate with that person. You can send love to people without liking them. Sending love means that you wish for that person good health, peace, joy, and happiness. The only prerequisite is that you must be sincere, and that is a conscious choice you have.

When you decide to forgive, you are really being selfish, because what you wish for the other, you are actually wishing for yourself. This is the real reason for thinking it and feeling it. As you think and feel, so you are. It is as simple as that.

Meditation can be a simple but effective way to bring about forgiveness in you. It can work miracles in your life as you practice it. Quiet your mind, relax, and let go. Be thankful for nature's love for you, and then affirm:

> *I fully and freely forgive (think of the name of the offender). I release that person mentally and spiritually. I completely forgive everything connected with that matter in question. I am free, and the person is free, and I feel wonderful. I release anybody and everybody who has ever hurt me, and I wish for each and everyone good health, happiness, peace, and joy. I do this freely, joyously, and lovingly. Whenever I think of the persons who hurt me, I say, "I have released you, and all the blessings of life are yours." I am free and you are free and it is wonderful.*

The real power of true forgiveness is that once you have forgiven the person, you don't need to repeat the whole affirmation. Whenever the person or the particular hurt happens to enter your mind, wish the delinquent well, and say, "Peace be with you." You will notice that after a few days, the thought of the experience will return less and less often, until it fades into nothingness.

Once you understand the creative power of your mind, you stop blaming other people and conditions for making your life difficult. You become aware that your own thoughts and feelings create your destiny. You also become aware that externals are not the causes and makers of your life and your experiences. To think that others can influence your happiness, that you must fight and oppose others for a living – all these ideas reveal their destructive nature when you understand that thoughts are things. This principle is clearly stated in the Bible: *"For as a man thinketh in his heart, so is he"* Proverbs 23:7

POINTS TO REMEMBER

1. Spiritual laws do not discriminate. Life seems to favour you once you begin to align yourself with the principles of harmony, health, joy, and peace.
2. Life never sends disease, sickness, accidents, or suffering. We bring these things on ourselves by our own negative destructive thinking, based upon the law: *As we sow, so shall we reap.*
3. Your concept of nature and spiritual laws is the most important thing in your life. If you really believe in a universe of abundance, support, harmony, and love, your subconscious mind will respond by bringing countless blessings to you.
4. Life holds no grudge against you. Life never condemns you. Life heals a cut on your hand, and forgives you if you burn your finger. It restores the part to wholeness and perfection.
5. Your guilt complex is a false concept of nature and life. Life does not punish or judge you. You do this to yourself by the subconscious effects of your false beliefs, negative thinking, and self-condemnation.
6. The forces of nature are not evil. The effect of their use depends on how you use the power within you. You can use electricity to kill

someone or to light the house. You can use water to drown a child or quench his thirst. Good and evil come right back to the thought and purpose in a person's own mind.

7. Life never punishes. People punish themselves by their false concept of life and the universe. Their thoughts are creative, and they create their own misery.

8. If someone criticizes you, and these faults are within you, give thanks, and appreciate the comments. This gives you the opportunity to correct the particular fault.

9. You cannot be hurt by criticism when you know that you are the master of your thoughts, reactions, and emotions. This gives you the opportunity to pray for and bless the other, thereby blessing yourself.

10. When you ask for guidance and right action, take what comes. Realize that it is good then there is no cause for self-pity, criticism, or hatred.

11. There is nothing good or bad, but thinking makes it so. There is no evil in the desire for food, sex, wealth, or true expression. It depends on how you use these urges, desires, or aspirations. Your desire for wealth can be met without robbing a bank.

12. To forgive is to give something for. Give love, peace, joy, wisdom, and all the blessings of life to others, until there is no sting left in your mind. This is the true test of forgiveness.

13. If someone has hurt you, lied about you, and has said all kinds of evil about you, is your thought of that person negative? If so, you have not yet forgiven. The roots of hatred are still in your subconscious mind, playing havoc with you. The only way to eliminate those roots is with love. Wish for the person all the blessings of life.

14. Resentment, hatred, and hostility are behind a host of problems. Forgive yourself and everybody else by pouring out love, life, joy, and goodwill to all who have hurt you. Continue until you can meet them in your mind and know that you are at peace with them.

We need to understand that all of our so-called problems are just opportunities for us to grow and to learn to change, and that most of them come from the vibrations we have been giving off. All we really need to do is change the way we think, be willing to dissolve the resentment, and be ready to forgive.

The best thing is to give:
to your enemy, forgiveness;
to an opponent, tolerance;
to a friend, your heart;
to your child, a good example;
to your father, deference;
to your mother, conduct that
will maker her proud of you;
to yourself, respect;
to all men, charity.

Francis Balfour

Chapter 15

Appreciation, Thankfulness, and Gratitude

*He who receives a good turn should never forget it;
he who does one should never remember it.*

Charron

NO MATTER WHOM we are or what our actions may say, we all want to be recognized and appreciated. It is as important in our life as food and drink is to our body. It is the fuel that keeps us going in life, motivates us and makes our life worth while. A famous coach once asked in an interview: "Why is it that the people who need love, appreciation, and understanding the most, usually deserve it the least?"

Jaime Escalante, the teacher on whom the movie "Stand and Deliver" was based, tells the following amazing story about a mistaken identity and the difference it made in a young man's life.

A teacher had two students in his class who were both named Johnny. One Johnny was an excellent student, a happy child, and always had his homework completed on time. The other Johnny was always in trouble, never had his work finished, and generally made the teacher's life miserable.

The night of their first PTA Open House of the year, a mother stayed after the meeting to ask about her son, Johnny, and how he was getting along in the class. Assuming it was the mother of the good Johnny, the teacher replied, "I can't tell you how much I appreciate him. I am so glad he's in my class."

The next day, for the first time all year, the problem Johnny had all his work done, he spoke up in class, and never once caused a disruption. He even volunteered to help another student. The teacher was astounded!

At the end of the day when everyone else had left, problem Johnny came up to the teacher and said, "My Mom told me what you said about me last night.

I have not ever had a teacher who wanted me in his class."

That Johnny became one of the best students the teacher ever had – and all because of a mistaken dose of appreciation! No matter who we are and what our situation in life is, we all want and need to be appreciated.

Be thankful for the wonderful gift of being able to serve humanity, your planet, and your God or your higher intelligence. Be thankful to the seeming roadblocks to your purpose. Remember, as Gandhi reminded us: "Divine guidance often comes when the horizon is the darkest."

Look at the entirety of your life, including all the people who have crossed your path. See all the jobs, successes, apparent failures, possessions, losses, wins – everything – from a perspective of gratitude. You are here for a reason: this is the key to feeling purposeful. Be grateful for the opportunity to live your life purposefully in tune with your higher intelligence. That is a lot to be grateful for. If you follow the instructions I give you, they will be certain to create perfect unity between your mind and your higher intelligence.

The whole process can be summed up in one word: *gratitude.*

First, you must believe that there is a higher intelligent substance from which all things proceed. Second, you must believe that this substance gives you everything you desire. And third, you must relate yourself to it through a feeling of deep and profound gratitude.

Many people who live their lives correctly in all other ways are kept in poverty by their lack of gratitude. After receiving one gift from God, they cut the wires connecting them to that creative source by failing to acknowledge this source. It is easy to understand that a soul who is always grateful lives in closer touch with God than one who never looks to him in thankful acknowledgement.

When good things come to us, the more gratefully we fix our minds on the supreme power, the more good things we will receive, and the more rapidly they will come. The reason for this is simply that the mental attitude of gratitude draws the mind into closer touch with the source from which the blessings come.

The thought that gratitude brings your whole mind closer to the creative energies of the universe may be a new thought for you. If so, consider it well and you will see that it is true. The good things you already possess have come to you because of certain laws. Gratitude will keep you in close harmony with creative thought and prevent you from becoming competitive. Gratitude alone can keep you looking toward the infinite and prevent you from falling back into the error of limiting beliefs.

If you want to achieve the results you seek, it is absolutely necessary to observe the Law of Gratitude, which is the natural principle that action and reaction are always equal and opposite. The grateful outreaching of your mind in thankful praise to the supreme power is liberation of force; it cannot fail to reach that to which it is addressed. And as a result, God responds with an instantaneous movement toward you.

Without gratitude, you will go back to being dissatisfied with things as they are. The moment you permit your mind to dwell with dissatisfaction upon things as they are, you begin to lose ground. You fix attention upon the poor, the common, and the mean. Then your mind takes the form of these things. You will then transmit these mental images. And the poor, the common, and the mean will come to you.

On the one hand, to permit your mind to dwell on the inferior is to become inferior and to surround yourself with inferior things. On the other hand, to fix your attention on the best is to surround yourself with the best and to become the best.

Therefore, it is necessary to cultivate the habit of being grateful for every good thing that comes to you – to give thanks continuously. Because all things have contributed to your advancement, you should include all things in your gratitude.

Do not waste time thinking or talking about the shortcomings or wrong actions of politicians or industry leaders. Their organization of the world has made your opportunity. All that you have received really has come to you because of them.

Do not rage against corrupt politicians. If it were not for politicians, we would fall into anarchy, and your opportunity would be greatly reduced. God has worked a long time and very patiently to bring us up to where we are in industry and government. And he is going right on with his work. I believe that he will do away with captains of industry, and politicians as soon as they can be spared. But in the meantime, they are necessary. Remember, they are helping to arrange the lines of transmission along which your healing and prosperity will come to you. Be grateful to them. This will bring you into a harmonious relationship with the good in everything, and the good in everything will move toward you.

Many people take the time to reach out and touch someone, possibly a perfect stranger. The following story is an example of how those who do selfless acts often reap rewards that cannot be measured.

He almost didn't see the old lady, stranded on the side of the road, but even in the dim light late in the afternoon, he could see she needed help. So he pulled up in front of her Mercedes and got out. His rusty Pontiac was still sputtering when he approached her.

Even with the smile on his face, she was worried. No one had stopped to help her, for the last hour or so. Was he going to hurt her? He didn't look safe; he looked poor and hungry and was wearing shabby clothes.

He could see that she was frightened, standing out there in the cold. He knew how she felt. It was that chill, which only fear can put into you. He said, "I'm here to help you, ma'am. Why don't you wait in the car where it's warm? By the way, my name is Brian Anderson."

Well, all she had was a flat tire, but for an old lady, that was bad enough. Brian crawled under the car looking for a place to put the jack, skinning his knuckles a time or two. Soon he was able to change the tire. But he had to get dirty, and his hands hurt. As he was tightening up the lug nuts, she rolled down the window and began to talk to him. She told him that she was from St. Louis and was only just passing through. She couldn't thank him enough for coming to her aid.

Brian just smiled as he closed her trunk. The lady asked how much she owed him. Any amount would have been alright with her. She already imagined all the awful things that could have happened, had he not stopped. Brian never thought twice about being paid. This was not a job to him. This was helping someone in need, and God knows there were plenty who had helped him in the past. He had lived his whole life that way, and it never occurred to him to act any other way.

He told the old lady that if she really wanted to pay him back, the next time she saw someone who needed help, she could give that person the help they needed, and Brian added, "And think of me."

He waited until she started her car and drove off. It had been a cold and depressing day, but he felt good as he headed for home, disappearing into the twilight.

A few miles down the road the lady saw a small cafe. She went in to grab a bite to eat, and take the chill off before she made the last leg of her trip home. It was a dingy looking restaurant. Outside were two old gas pumps. The whole scene was unfamiliar to her.

The waitress came over and brought a clean towel to wipe her wet hair. She had a sweet smile, one that being on her feet for the whole day couldn't erase. The lady noticed that although the waitress was nearly eight months pregnant, she didn't let the strain and aches of her job change her attitude. The old lady wondered how someone who had so little could be so giving to a stranger, and then she remembered Brian.

After the lady finished her meal, she paid with a hundred dollar bill. The waitress quickly went to get change for her hundred dollar bill, but the old lady had slipped out the door. She was gone by the time the waitress came back with the change. The waitress wondered where the lady could be.

Then she noticed something written on the napkin. There were tears in her eyes when she read what the woman had written: "You don't owe me anything. I have been there too. Somebody once helped me out, the way I'm helping you now. If you really want to pay me back, here is what you do: Do not let this chain of love end with you."

Under the napkin were four more hundred dollar bills.

Well, there were tables to clear, sugar bowls to fill, and people to serve, but the waitress made it through another day. That night when she got home from work and climbed into bed, she was thinking about the money and what the lady had written. How could she have known how much she and her husband needed it? With the baby due next month, it was going to be hard.

She knew how worried her husband was, and as he lay sleeping next to her, she gave him a soft kiss on his shoulder and whispered soft and low, "Everything's going to be all right. I love you, Brian Anderson."

WISHING

Do you wish the world were better? Let me tell you what to do:
Set a watch upon your actions; always keep them straight and true.
Rid your mind of selfish motives; let your thoughts be clean and high,
You can make a little Eden of the space you occupy.

Do you wish the world were wiser? Well suppose you make a start,
By accumulating wisdom, in the scrapbook of your heart,
Do not waste one page on folly, live to learn and learn to live,
If you want to give men knowledge, you must get it where you give.

Do you wish the world were happy? Then remember day by day,
Just to scatter seeds of kindness as you pass along the way.
For the pleasure of the many may be often traced to one,
As the hand that plants the acorn shelters armies from the sun.

Ella Wheeler Wilcox

Postscript

The most beautiful and most profound emotion we can experience is the sensation of the mystical. It is the dower of all true science. He to whom this emotion is a stranger, who can no long wonder and stand rapt in awe, is as good as dead. To know that what is impenetrable to us really exists, manifesting itself as the highest wisdom and the most radiant beauty which our dull faculties can comprehend only in their most primitive forms – this knowledge, this feeling is at the center of true religiousness.

Albert Einstein

May you stand in awe at the perfection of the universe and marvel at your part in the beauty and magnificence surrounding you.

May you look deeply within your own soul and see the perfection that you are – the reflection of Infinite Intelligence.

You are a child of the universe and deserve to be here. Listen closely to the still, small voice within and have the courage to act upon its quiet, loving promptings and guidance. Listen closely to the wisdom of your heart and obey.

As you look upon your fellow men and women, see them as a mirror of yourself; each of you is here to reflect your compassion and love to each other.

My greatest wish for you is that you will experience the blessings and healing power of the greatest force of all – unconditional love.

May you always be thankful and be healed.

Axel Menzefricke

References

Anderson, Greg. *50 Essential Things to Do When the Doctor Says It's Cancer.* Plume Book, 1993.

Dwoskin, Hale. *The Sedona Method: Your Key to Lasting Happiness, Success, Peace and Emotional Well-Being.* Sedona AZ: Sedona Press, 2003

Dyer, Wayne W. *Manifest Your Destiny: The Nine Spiritual Principles for getting Everything You Want.* Harper Collins, 1997.

Dyer, Wayne W. *The Power of Intention: Learning to Co-Create your World your Way.* Hay House, 2004.

Foundation for Inner Peace. *A Course in Miracles.* Internet resource, available at http://www.acim.org/.

Hawkins, David. *Power vs. Force: The Hidden Determinants of Human Behavior.* Hay House, 2002; Veritas, 2001.

Hay, Louise L. *The Power is Within You.* Hay House, 1991

Hay, Louise L. *You Can Heal Your Life.* Hay House, 1987.

Hicks, Jerry and Esther. *Ask and It is Given: Learning to Manifest your Desires.* Hay House, 2004.

Hill, Napoleon. *Think and Grow Rich*. Fawcett Crest, 1983.

Murphy, Joseph. *The Power of your Subconscious Mind*. Prentice-Hall, 1988.

Myss, Caroline. *Anatomy of the Spirit: The Seven Stages of Power and Healing*. Harmony Books, 1996.

Nightingale – Conant Corporation. Offers a wide variety of audio cassettes on
living fully. Available online at http://www.nightingale.com/.

Proctor, Bob. *You Were Born Rich: Now You can Discover and Develop those Riches*. Life Success Productions, 1997.

Siegel, Bernie S. *Peace, Love, and Healing: Body-Mind Communication and the Path to Self-Healing*. Walker, 1990.

Toastmasters International. A non profit organization that teaches self confidence, communication skills, and leadership qualities. Information available online at www.toastmasters.org.

Trudeau, Kevin. *Natural Cures "They" Don't Want You to Know About*. Alliance, 2005.

Vitale, Joe. *The Attractor Factor: 5 Easy Steps for Creating Wealth (or anything else) from the Inside Out*. John Wiley, 2005.

Workshop / Keynote Topics:

Axel has built a reputation for giving thought-provoking, compassionate, and inspiring presentations to help people unleash their personal power.

REGAINING YOUR HEALTH – *Surviving and thriving in spite of illness.*
Through his story of personal triumph, Axel will share the steps needed to take control of your health. Accept your reality; change your attitudes and beliefs. And through the power of affirmation, meditation, and visualization, you can learn to adjust your lifestyle.

NEVER GIVE UP! – *Overcoming fear.*
We all have fear. It is part of life. Discover what holds you back and gain the tools to move ahead. You can attain the health, wealth, and success you desire.

CREATE THE LIFE YOU WANT – *Tools for making powerful choices.*
Axel has changed careers six times in his life and now is living his dream as a motivational speaker. He will guide you in determining what will bring you the most happiness and success – a path to celebrate your uniqueness.

BALANCE – *The secret to happiness in life*
Learn what to balance, how to balance it, and how to achieve happiness and success *for you* – useful information for avoiding burnout, illness, and relationship problems.

Axel Menzefricke, ACS Toastmaster

Helping people use their own power to heal themselves and create the lives they want.

Throughout his life, Axel has had the courage, strength, and determination to recreate his life and overcome the obstacles, illnesses, and challenges that hold others back. He worked for 20 years in the hospitality industry as a Certified Chef, Administrator and Hotel Manager, before becoming a freelance Photographer and then Retoucher in a commercial studio.

Diagnosed with colon cancer at the age of 35, he had the malignant polyps removed, only to have the cancer metastasize to his liver 6 months later. Reflecting on the death of his father, from liver cancer at the age of 60, Axel realized that his attitudes and thinking patterns were similar to those of his father. He decided to take anger management classes, alternative healing methods, lectures and seminars. By reading books from Dr. Wayne Dyer, Louise L. Hay, and Marianne Williamson, he discovered a spiritual path. The cancer disappeared and never came back.

Axel is determined to share his lessons with others. He has a passion for helping people use their own power to heal themselves and create the lives they want.